"In a world seemingly convinced that our fragmented, lonely, isolated existences are not only inevitable but good, *Becoming God's Family* offers a refreshing and hopeful description of the meaning and significance of the family of God. Carmen Joy Imes has given the church the gift of a rousing call to take seriously our belonging to one another. Even those skeptical of the church will find in these pages a compelling vision of Christian faith that not only teaches us right doctrine but envelops us into a family."

Kaitlyn Schiess, author of *The Ballot and the Bible*

"Carmen Joy Imes's *Becoming God's Family* is a breath of clean and hopeful air! She shows us why God, in his sheer brilliance, would do much of his work in our life through a broken, slow, imperfect, cumbersome, and at times frustrating community of people called the church. Indeed, as the author shows, the church still matters—perhaps more than ever before. This book will bring waves of healing to God's people."

A. J. Swoboda, associate professor of Bible and theology at Bushnell University and author of *The Gift of Thorns*

"This is a stirring book, beautifully written and rich on every page. Bringing the Scriptures and our lives together, this book has been needed for a long time. Many of us have longed for a book that explores the family inside the biblical tradition. This book is a gift to ministers, practical theologians, and biblical scholars."

Andrew Root, professor and Carrie Olson Baalson Chair of Youth and Family Ministry at Luther Seminary and author of the Ministry in A Secular Age series

"In this volume, all the obvious passion Carmen Joy Imes has for the church is wrapped up together with all her academic rigor to produce a stunningly good study of our roots. By helping us better understand how we began, Carmen shows us what we can become and how we can best belong. This book is for everyone who loves the church . . . or wants to."

Carolyn Moore, bishop for the Global Methodist Church

"One of the longest studies ever conducted on human life—the Harvard Study of Adult Development—found the top factor in living a long, happy life is deep relationships in a healthy community. As believers we know this is near to the heart of God, who gave us the church as a spiritual family. Carmen Joy Imes gives a strong and needed call to this community in our land marked today by individualism and division."

Ed Stetzer, dean of the Talbot School of Theology

"*Becoming God's Family* weaves together God's design for the redeemed community. This biblical tapestry holds together beautifully, even if a thread or two may be a bit stretched. This well-informed and practical book issues a compelling and challenging call to embrace God's love for the church."

Daniel J. Treier, Gunther H. Knoedler Professor of Theology and PhD program director at Wheaton College

"Carmen Joy Imes masterfully communicates the contours of the Creator's grand narrative to fashion a family of humans who live out their vocation as God's image to a world that desperately needs the author of life. *Becoming God's Family* does not shy away from hard-to-swallow stories within the Scriptures while simultaneously pointing towards the promised future of a multiethnic and multicultural family of God. Imes offers graceful reminders and truthful challenges, emphasizing that while God's family awaits the renewal of all things, we testify to what God has already accomplished."

Mike Chu, academic director at AWKNG School of Theology

"When first starting our church, I was told that learning to be the church would be our biggest challenge. More than gathering unchurched people, starting ministries, or leading Sunday worship, growing into our identity as God's people had to be our priority. I needed this book back then! Expertly working her way through the Old Testament into the Gospels and Epistles, Carmen Joy Imes reveals that it has always been God's desire to form disparate and diverse people into a family who reflect his glory. Accessible and inspiring, *Becoming God's Family* is a beautiful vision for being the church."

David W. Swanson, pastor and author of *Plundered*

"I loved her first two books, but this one is my favorite by far. For a culture infected with a nigh pathological commitment to polarization, *Becoming God's Family* offers the antidote. The church is still the most beautiful thing out there. Thank you, Carmen Joy Imes, for reminding us of this."

Evan Wickham, lead pastor of Park Hill Church

"*In Becoming God's Family*, Carmen Joy Imes holds out hope for the church, a vision for a safe and healthy church, and a reason to stay. As an expert scholar, Imes skillfully walks us through the Old Testament, combining analysis of the biblical text with compelling personal stories. She shows us that churches are not predestined to repeat the harm that they have done. Rather, together, we can embody the diversity, justice, and healing of the kingdom of God. A must-read!"

Mark Glanville, author of *Preaching in a New Key* and *Improvising Church*

FOREWORD BY ESAU McCAULLEY

BECOMING GOD'S FAMILY

WHY THE CHURCH STILL MATTERS

CARMEN JOY IMES

ivp
Academic

An imprint of InterVarsity Press
Downers Grove, Illinois

InterVarsity Press
P.O. Box 1400 | Downers Grove, IL 60515-1426
ivpress.com | email@ivpress.com

InterVarsity Press® is the publishing division of InterVarsity Christian Fellowship/USA®. For more information, visit intervarsity.org.

All Scripture quotations, unless otherwise indicated, are taken from The Holy Bible, New International Version®, NIV®. Copyright © 1973, 1978, 1984, 2011 by Biblica, Inc.™ Used by permission of Zondervan. All rights reserved worldwide. www.zondervan.com. The "NIV" and "New International Version" are trademarks registered in the United States Patent and Trademark Office by Biblica, Inc.™

While any stories in this book are true, some names and identifying information may have been changed to protect the privacy of individuals.

Figure 10.1 taken from Unsplash.com

The publisher cannot verify the accuracy or functionality of website URLs used in this book beyond the date of publication.

Cover design: Faceout Studio
Interior design: Daniel van Loon
Images: Getty Images: © CSA Images; © RobinOlimb / DigitalVision Vectors

ISBN 978-1-5140-1032-7 (print) | ISBN 978-1-5140-1033-4 (digital)

Printed in the United States of America ♾

Library of Congress Cataloging-in-Publication Data
A catalog record for this book is available from the Library of Congress.

31 30 29 28 27 26 25 | 13 12 11 10 9 8 7 6 5 4 3 2 1

For Calvary Mennonite Church and Roca de Salvación,

now united to become Living Stone Bible Church.

Your faithfulness to God and each other inspires me.

Thanks for loving us like family for so many years.

Para la Iglesia Menonita del Calvario y Roca de Salvación,

ahora unidas como Living Stone Bible Church.

Su fidelidad a Dios y a los demás me inspira.

Gracias por amarnos como familia durante tantos años.

*So now you Gentiles are no longer strangers and foreigners.
You are citizens along with all of God's holy people. You are
members of God's family. Together, we are his house, built
on the foundation of the apostles and the prophets. And the
cornerstone is Christ Jesus himself. We are carefully joined
together in him, becoming a holy temple for the Lord. Through
him you Gentiles are also being made part of this dwelling
where God lives by his Spirit.*

(EPHESIANS 2:19-22 NLT)

CONTENTS

FOREWORD

Esau McCaulley

Jonathan Blanchard Associate Professor of New
Testament and Public Theology, Wheaton College

I have never written a trilogy, but I have read many and watched
more than my fair share on television. A good trilogy must have a
strong first entry, or the audience won't want to stick around.
Dr. Carmen Imes got off to that great start with *Bearing God's Name:
Why Sinai Still Matters*. There she explained the continuing relevance
of the Old Testament and in particular our call to bear God's name
(that is, to represent him well) wherever we go.

A good trilogy needs a second book that builds on the work of
the first but explores interesting territory in its own right. Again
Dr. Imes does this in *Being God's Image: Why Creation Still Matters*. There she tackled a central teaching of the first book of
the Bible that has serious implications for how Christians live in
the world—namely, the belief that every person is created in
God's image.

A trilogy must also land the plane. The third entry needs to say something that makes the investment of time worth our commitment over a period of years between the entries. I am not sure if Carmen is done with the series (I hope not). But in any case, readers who have been around since the beginning will not be disappointed. Those who have not read the previous books can also jump in right here and completely understand this book's central ideas. *Becoming God's Family: Why the Church Still Matters* stands on its own, but it may inspire readers to consult her previous work.

What can readers expect to find in the excellent *Becoming God's Family*? First, readers will find that Dr. Imes has the rare gift of being a biblical scholar that can speak to the academy, clergy, and people in the pews at the same time. In this book she demonstrated her ability to translate a lifetime of learning into accessible writing without being simplistic or assuming that her audience cannot handle complex ideas. As someone who pastors and teaches at a divinity school, I found myself thinking that ideas found in this book would work great in a lecture *and* a sermon.

Second, the content of *Becoming God's Family* is something of a whirlwind tour of the entire biblical narrative with the aim of figuring out what it means to be God's family (the church) and why remaining a part of that family matters. Sometimes Carmen helps us learn through examples worthy of imitation. Other times we are formed through avoiding the failures of biblical characters.

This is not some dry study of "family" or "church" across the canon. *Becoming God's Family* has one foot in the worlds of the Old and New Testament and the other in our modern context. She understands that we live in a context where, for a variety of reasons, people are skeptical of the church. She addresses those concerns head on chapter after chapter. But she does not stop at lament nor does she despair that we can be better.

Instead of rejecting the church, Dr. Imes posits a way of healing it, using the lessons of Scripture to make it what it was always meant to be: a people made in God's image, bearing God's name, as God's family on mission to extend that family to all who would answer the call of the beloved Son.

INTRODUCTION

Why does the White Witch woo Edmund away from his siblings? Four children travel to Narnia in C. S. Lewis's classic fantasy series, but only one of them meets the witch. The adventures of the Pevensie children begin in *The Lion, the Witch, and the Wardrobe*, where quite by accident they discover another world. In Narnia, Aslan, a great lion, is the rightful ruler over a kingdom of talking animals who are under the control of an evil usurper. However, the children are not merely spectators but participants in this parallel world. As the White Witch knows from the ancient prophecies, all four thrones in the castle at Cair Paravel must be occupied by sons of Adam and daughters of Eve, that is, by humans. Together, the humans are to exercise dominion on Aslan's behalf. This is why the witch targets Edmund, enticing him to come to her castle and holding him captive there. As long as his throne is empty at Cair Paravel, the rule of Aslan will be compromised. To exercise a dominion that ensures the flourishing of Narnia and the unbroken rule of Aslan is a group project.

Aslan's whereabouts are often unknown and his comings and goings unpredictable. The moment he arrives, winter begins to melt into spring as all creation warms to his presence. Aslan gathers Peter, Susan, and Lucy along with all those loyal to him to prepare for the inevitable battle with the White Witch. Aslan shatters the witch's power, not by killing her but by offering himself on their behalf. The children join Aslan in the battle against the witch and her minions as they liberate all of Narnia, including Edmund.

The siblings joyfully reunite as subjects of Aslan, who appoints them to rule Narnia on his behalf. Each one plays an essential role in the administration of Aslan's kingdom. Each offers something unique and essential. The children sit on their four thrones at Cair Paravel while Narnia enjoys a long season of peace and prosperity, until one day the kings and queens of Narnia stumble on the wardrobe through which they entered that world. Drawn by a distant memory, they walk through the portal and find themselves back in England.

I didn't know it then, but I walked through a wardrobe (of sorts) as a child of eleven. It was a Tuesday evening in the temperamental Colorado spring. My dad and I entered the doors of Third Christian Reformed Church and climbed the stairs to the second floor. It was strange to be in a mostly darkened church, absent the Sunday morning crowds. We walked down the dim hallway to the pastor's study. Reverend Nydam let me sit on one of the ornate chairs to wait while our church's leaders—he and Reverend Kok and the elders and deacons (including my dad)—convened around an enormous oval table in the boardroom across the hall. Eventually, they called for me and I entered the room. The wooden armchair at the head of the table was empty. They had saved it for me. I remember feeling so small perched on that chair, my legs dangling.

My memory is fuzzy at this point. I mostly recall the regal curves of the carved table pedestal. I must have been too shy to maintain eye contact. The men took turns asking me questions about my understanding of the Scriptures and the catechism (our church's doctrinal standards) and the Christian life. They were examining me to see whether my professed faith in Jesus was sound. Time stood still. I don't know whether they spoke with me for ten minutes or an hour. I was intimidated. What eleven-year-old wouldn't be? But I was also certain. I knew that I wanted to spend the rest of my life following Jesus. My parents had baptized me as an infant. The next step was to make a public profession of faith during the church service. That would make me an official member of the congregation and qualify me to participate in Communion.

Most young people who grew up in our church officially joined when they were older, perhaps in high school. To my parents' dismay, when my grandparents found out I had already decided to declare my faith publicly, they shook their heads in disapproval. They were sure that I was too young to understand the gravity of this decision. I'd already belonged to Jesus for as long as I could remember, so I couldn't see any reason to wait, and neither could my parents. That's how I found myself in that boardroom on a Tuesday evening, an eleven-year-old girl on an oversized throne with more than a dozen men in business suits focused on me. I wanted to belong to the church. I was all in.

I have never regretted that decision. I entered the room with a desire to declare my faith in Jesus, and I walked out as a member of God's forever family. I had been adopted. To throw in my lot with these men (and all the other members) was my destiny. Those adult men around the table had mysteriously become my brothers in Christ, and I was their sister. I didn't recognize then the significance of the chair I occupied in that boardroom. Like the thrones in Narnia, the church was incomplete without me. On June 4, 1989, I stood before our entire congregation in the Sunday morning service to declare that I belonged to Jesus and to his church. I have belonged ever since. And while I have moved over a dozen times, in each place I have found a new church family in which to grow and serve, love and be loved.

Many who are raised in the church find their faith unraveling over time. Maybe you've struggled to square what you heard from the pulpit with what you learned in the high school or college classroom. Maybe someone pulled back the curtain so you could see that the morality of your parents and their tribe was riddled with hypocrisy or had more to do with politics than the Bible. Maybe as you've gotten older the simple lessons you learned in Sunday school seemed unable to hold the weight of the grim complexities of life. Maybe the adults in church who were supposed to protect you caused harm instead. If so, you are not alone.

I'm forty-seven now. A lot has transpired for me since that day in 1989. I have outgrown some of my childhood certainty about the way the world works. But I have never outgrown the church. Eventually our family began attending a new church, where we discovered new dimensions of God we had been missing. I've had periods of frustration and disappointment over Christian subculture. But although my theology has shifted on various issues over these decades, I remain convinced that the Bible is God's self-revelation to us and the foundation of the life we're meant to share. The overarching narrative of the Bible is singularly focused on forming a faithful community of people who worship and wait for God while carrying out his mission in the world. Leaning into this vision hasn't always been easy, but the church has been a source of deep and lasting joy for me. This book is not a memoir, but it would be fair to call it a love story.

I am persuaded, passionately so, that the church matters. It still matters, even after scandalous headlines and hurtful experiences, after waves of deconstruction and disillusionment, after a global pandemic that upended our routines, and after the political polarization that resulted. We still need the church. We need the church *because* of these things. The church is riddled with problems because we bring ourselves to it, and we're often a mess. It carries a hefty laundry list of wrongs done and rights left undone, but it also carries beauty and goodness. Tucked away in its history is a litany of stories in which people experienced help, healing, and transformation, people

> The overarching narrative of the Bible is singularly focused on forming a faithful community of people who worship and wait for God while carrying out his mission in the world.

whose destinies shifted as they caught a glimpse of the glory of God at work in ordinary gatherings made up of all sorts of people, people who were surprised to discover a place to truly belong.

But what *is* the church? Is it a building? A weekly gathering? A spiritual family? A shorthand way of referring to all believers in Jesus through the ages? It is all these things and more. We could use the word *church* to refer to a local assembly of believers or the universal body of Christ that spans history. This book is about both.

DEFINING CHURCH

Many people assume that the church started on the day of Pentecost, when God poured out the Holy Spirit on the believers who were gathered in Jerusalem (Acts 2). That was indeed a special day that inaugurated a new era, but technically speaking, the church started much earlier than that. Peter speaks of the followers of Jesus as standing in continuity with the covenant people of the Old Testament, using the same titles to describe them: "holy nation," "chosen people," "royal priesthood," and "treasured representatives" (1 Peter 2:9-10, author's translation). I have written more about this continuity in *Bearing God's Name*.

The Greek word usually translated "church" in the New Testament is *ekklēsia*. *Ekklēsia* is not an abstract word that points to an individual's membership in a community. *Ekklēsia* refers more concretely to an active gathering, usually for political or religious purposes but sometimes for a military event. *Ekklēsia* can refer to a gathering of citizens (Acts 19:32), the assembly of ancient Israelites (1 Kings 8:14), a local Christian community meeting for worship (Romans 16:5), or even the global body of believers (Ephesians 1:22). The Greek translation of the Old Testament uses *ekklēsia* regularly to refer to Israelites assembled in God's presence. For example, Deuteronomy 9:10 speaks of the *ekklēsia*—the assembly of Israelites gathered at the base of Mount Sinai, awaiting God's instruction. That background made it the ideal word to describe New Testament believers, filled with the Holy Spirit and gathered to worship God.

We could call the church an *incarnational community* informed by the Scriptures.[1] By *incarnational* I mean that the church bears embodied witness to Christ in a particular place. Christianity is not just a theological idea. It takes shape in actual buildings where people show up and participate. Christians become an intercultural and intergenerational family around the Communion table, where we celebrate Christ's self-giving love, and in the trenches of daily life, where we serve one another and our neighbors.

Evangelical Christians tend to define ourselves by the doctrinal beliefs we hold in common. However, evangelicals are known by others for our worship gatherings more than for our doctrine. Judging from stock photos in online articles, evangelicals are people who assemble to sing and to hear a sermon.[2] So while the church is more than a building, the building or meeting place signals the most defining feature of the church: a local community that gathers for worship in a particular place. The Sunday (or Saturday) gathering is not the sum total of the church. It operates all week long in hospital visits, Bible studies, spiritual conversations, prayer meetings, food pantries, tutoring sessions, and friends having coffee.

Theologian Andrew Root offers a robust vision of the church, insisting that it is neither an affinity group nor an entrepreneurial venture. Instead, the church facilitates shared participation in the life of God by the Spirit, which is to say that when we gather for worship, we gather around a transcendent mystery that we can neither control nor fully understand. Root explains, "The church is the community that reminds the world that God is God, seeking to commune with a God who is other than us."[3]

The church was never meant to become an empire, a program, a personality cult, or an entertaining escape from boredom on the one hand or suffering on the other. The mission of the church is and always has been to bear witness to something outside itself by waiting and praying with the world for an encounter with God. We gather to seek God's presence. On our best days, we recognize that we cannot manufacture this ourselves but must simply be ready to receive.

This book began around a fire pit on a camping trip. As I recall, we had just toasted marshmallows, and someone was passing around a package of dried and seasoned crickets for the more daring among us to try. The conversation turned to spiritual things. A member of our extended family expressed that he believed in Jesus but saw no use for the church. He just didn't need it (and didn't want anyone else telling him what to do). He and God were doing just fine on their own. It occurred to me then that the reason for church wasn't obvious. Someone needed to make a case for it.

> The mission of the church is and always has been to bear witness to something outside itself by waiting and praying with the world for an encounter with God.

For those of us deeply shaped by a world saturated with self-determination, the logic of church may seem foreign. We may have joined a congregation only for what we thought the church could do for us. If we treat the church as a self-help club, we are bound to be disappointed because the calling of the church is not to help each of us to live our best life now. Instead, the church is designed to decenter each one of us, to testify that we are not enough on our own and that we do not have what it takes alone to fix what is broken. The church testifies that we are dependent on a God we cannot control. In a world of same-day shipping and instant downloads, gathering to wait with others for God presents a significant challenge.

Perhaps we'd rather skip to the front of the line or embark on a personal quest for fulfillment. Instead, God calls us to be with and for each other. He invites us to serve and be served, to let our lives become entangled in healthy ways with other followers of Jesus. As members of his church family, God offers us not just friendship but siblingship. I become your sister in Christ.

Some of us come from collectivist cultures where loyalties to our people run deep. For us to form meaningful bonds with a new community of faith may be as big of a challenge as it was for believers in the first century. Putting the family of faith *first* comes at a high cost in relation to our natural families. When he asks, "Who is my mother, and who are my brothers?" (Matthew 12:48), Jesus questions our family loyalties and asks us to give up everything to follow him. In Jesus we discover a connection that is deeper and truer than the blood that runs through our veins. Knowing this has the power to change everything.

Of course, the vision I offer here is not always reality. Some of us have invested deeply in the church, believing it matters. But we became disillusioned when the church began to look more like a social club or a business network than a worshiping community, or when our leaders became more concerned about their platform than God's.

But God has no plan B. The church is inefficient and awkward, imperfect, and sometimes wrong-headed. But it's utterly irreplaceable. In the pages of this book, I hope to convince you of that. Our journey through Scripture will illuminate stories you might not have noticed before. All of them illustrate the truth that when God's people gather to wait for him to act, we experience unimaginable blessing.

Community is also undeniably messy. When a church fails to meet our expectations, the sense of betrayal and disappointment can run deep, sometimes for very good reasons. This community is meant to walk with us through our most difficult challenges

> The church is inefficient and awkward, imperfect, and sometimes wrong-headed. But it's utterly irreplaceable.

and encourage us on the journey. If we feel invisible or—even worse—mistreated, it's natural to want to rush to the exit and never return.

Just ask the young pastoral intern who was hired to bring solid biblical teaching to the youth but was later let go because he didn't plan enough fun activities.

Just ask the gifted woman with a seminary degree who feels a deep sense of calling to preach but the only place she is allowed to teach is children's Sunday school.

Just ask the man who was invited to be an elder but then regularly excluded from major decisions because he didn't speak in tongues and therefore wasn't considered "Spirit-filled."

Just ask the woman who discovered her husband was abusing their children, but when she sought safety, her pastor publicly condemned her for lack of faithfulness to her marriage.

Just ask the couple who invested thirty years in their congregation, but when they stopped attending, nobody even seemed to notice.

Just ask the woman who recalls her pastor telling her to be like Mary,
submitting herself to God as he stole her innocence and shattered
her future.

As Russell Moore, a former Southern Baptist leader and current
editor in chief of *Christianity Today*, explains, "We see now young
evangelicals walking away from evangelicalism not because they do
not believe what the church teaches, but because they believe the
church itself does not believe what the church teaches."[4]

Maybe this is you. Whether you're among the 16 percent of Ameri-
cans who have already stopped attending church, or whether you're
on the verge of leaving, wondering whether it's worth the heartache
to keep trying, this book is for you.[5] I have not seen what you've seen
or experienced the hurt you've experienced. You may have very good
reasons to be disillusioned with your church. What I know is that
we aren't built to navigate this life without a spiritual family to nour-
ish our faith. We need each other.

My hope is that this book will rekindle your desire to seek fellowship with other believers, even when doing so is not easy. I don't
advocate that we ignore abuse or false teaching. We should take both
very seriously. But in those cases, we can renew our search for a
healthy community of believers who have gathered around the
mystery of Christ's first coming in anticipation of his return. We
need not insist that they see the world exactly as we do, voting for
our favorite candidate or reading every Bible passage the same way.
Our core commitments to Christ and his Word can tolerate a host
of other differences.

Like the first two books in this trilogy, *Being God's Image* and
Bearing God's Name, the book you hold in your hands is a work of
biblical theology written for the church about the church. You don't
have to be a scholar to understand it. And you don't have to have
read the other books for this one to make sense (though I hope you

do!). We'll be following the community of faith through the entire Bible. Along the way, we'll discover that God delights to break into this world from beyond so he can dwell among his people. When God's people gather, God often shows up. When we stop meeting together, we miss out on the possibility of the presence of God mediated in part by our brothers and sisters in Christ.

The church is a multiethnic and multicultural assembly of believers spanning history that God has called into fellowship with Christ and with one another. We gather regularly to consider the teachings of the Bible and to orient our lives around God's coming kingdom. Together we wait for God to make all things new, and we bear witness to the world of what God has already done. New Testament authors use various metaphors to describe the church. We are the body of Christ. We are built into a temple. We are siblings, members of God's family, and fellow heirs of his promises. We are citizens of an alternative kingdom. We'll explore several of these metaphors as we trace the theme of God's presence in the community of faith throughout the Bible.

THE PEOPLE WHO WAIT

I remember a fascinating class I took with a beloved professor in college: Advanced Pedagogy. I wanted to become a teacher, so I was eager to soak it all in. We were learning best practices for teaching from a man who was himself a master teacher. One day, our professor broke us into groups and gave us challenges to complete. The task involved spatial reasoning and problem solving, which came naturally for me. To be painfully honest, I was thinking how lucky my group was to have me because we had a good shot at finishing first. In moments, I had completed the task and flagged down our professor. What happened next is forever etched in my memory. "I didn't ask you to complete this quickly, Carmen. I asked you to complete it *together*."

I'm sure my face reddened in shame. I had failed completely because I had misunderstood the goal. Our aim was not efficiency but cooperation. By completing the challenge myself, I had robbed myself and the rest of the group of the joy of discovery and the satisfaction of working together.

Many of the stories in the Bible (and frankly, in the church today) give evidence of a similar misdiagnosis. When we misunderstand human purpose, imagining ourselves to be on a solo quest for self-actualization or trying to prove our value through our achievements, we miss out on the community God designed for us to enjoy and the divine empowerment that comes as a result.

We're going to trek through Scripture in this book to see how it signals our need for community. Before we do, it's helpful to jump ahead to the New Testament to consider Jesus' last words to his followers before his ascension into heaven. Doing so will sharpen our focus on our shared purpose. Christians believe that Jesus is exhibit A demonstrating God's supernatural presence among us. By becoming human, Jesus, the second member of the Trinity, fully entered our world, experiencing all we do and transforming our ability to commune with God. His resurrection was a great victory over sin and death, but his ascension represented a loss of his presence. God-with-us vacated the scene, leaving us-without-God. This is why Jesus instructed his followers, "Do not leave Jerusalem, but *wait for the gift my Father promised*, which you have heard me speak about. For John baptized with water, but in a few days you will be baptized with the Holy Spirit" (Acts 1:4-5). God's presence would be available to us in a new way.

The vocation of God's people had always been to wait for God's promise to be fulfilled. Here, even after Jesus' momentous death and resurrection, God's people had more waiting to do. That waiting would turn into witnessing: "It is not for you to know the times or dates the Father has set by his own authority. But you will receive power when the Holy Spirit comes on you; and *you will be my witnesses* in Jerusalem, and in all Judea and Samaria, and to the ends of the earth" (Acts 1:7-8).

The people who gathered to wait for God's presence would bear witness to it throughout the earth.

We'll return to this story in chapter eight to consider how it turns out, but I want us to have Jesus' final instructions in mind as we think about the vocation of the people of God throughout the Scriptures. We'll find that in every age, the people of God are the people who gather to wait for him to act. Our waiting is active, not passive, but collectively we recognize that without God we cannot accomplish what he intends. Waiting together is our most important job. You can imagine how things might go wrong if we didn't know this—if we thought that it was up to each of us individually to figure out a way to thrive. Now we turn back to Genesis to see how the story begins.

BEING OR BECOMING GOD'S FAMILY?

If you've already read *Being God's Image*, you know that I insist that every human being is the image of God. Being God's image is our human identity, and it cannot be lost, diminished, or destroyed. Our identity as God's image has strong vocational implications. The image of God is the basis for our vocation as rulers over creation, and it also qualifies us as part of God's royal family.

Perhaps that makes the title of this book somewhat puzzling. How can we *become* God's family if we already are? The fact is that most humans are estranged from their Creator. We haven't lost our status as God's image, but we haven't oriented our lives around that identity. What we all need is a radical reconciliation with our Heavenly Father that results in an equally radical reorientation toward each other as siblings in God's family.

E. Randolph Richards and Richard James explain, "The early church lived in a collective culture where kinship was a basic building block of society and family defined what it meant to be me."[a] As we'll see, Jesus and Paul both repeatedly use kinship language to describe fellow believers who are not blood related. This would have come as quite a shock to first-century believers. Richards and James continue, "Ancient Mediterranean cultures would not have encouraged redefining family. It was such a strange concept that Paul needed to use a metaphor they would understand: adoption."[b] Marriage allied two families with each other, but it did not supersede blood relationships. The sibling relationship was even stronger than marriage. Adoption was the only way someone could officially become a sibling and heir in the Greco-Roman world.

Biological children do not need to be adopted by their biological parents. If all humanity is already part of God's family, then adoption is not necessary. However, *adoption* is the best word available to Paul to describe to a collectivist audience the radical change in allegiance that comes with faith in Christ. He is calling for men and women to consider fellow followers of Jesus as their new family.

In other words, Paul uses the metaphor of adoption to emphasize the dramatic reorientation of priorities and allegiances that come with membership in the family of faith. So, while every human is already technically part of God's royal family, the task of discipleship is learning to live like it is true.

Becoming God's family is not simply a heartwarming way of talking about belonging to the church. It requires us to rethink our finances, our time, our space, and our priorities. To take part in this community that waits together for God to act will cost us everything. But it's 100 percent worth it.

1

THE FAMILY OF
ABRAHAM

OUR HUMAN FAMILY

When God created and brought order to the world, he appointed humans to rule over creation on his behalf. He blessed us, encouraging us to multiply and fill the earth so that God's presence would be felt in every place. The first thing in creation that was *not* good was loneliness. The first human was alone until God created a partner, an ally, who could work with him side by side. Together they would govern creation, and together they would produce offspring to be part of God's big family. This would only go well if they oriented themselves toward God and did things God's way.

I write more about our human identity as God's image and our vocation to rule the earth in *Being God's Image*. The Bible teaches that every human is the image of God. We represent God's presence to the rest of creation. God delegates to us the tasks of creating and maintaining order in the world. Nothing we do can disqualify us from this task, and we cannot lose this identity as God's image. It's the single most important thing about us. But when we live as if it's not true, everything goes wonky.

In the plot line of the Bible, God's good creation and his appointment for humans to rule on his behalf gives way to disaster. Although God designs humans to flourish in community with one another, with himself, and with the world he made, humans chose (and keep choosing) their own path, seeking autonomy from God. Genesis 3 tells the story of the human couple conspiring to make their own way in the world, rather than doing things God's way. They think they can find wisdom outside God's command instead of depending on God to teach them. They hide from God and blame each other, and as a result they experience a life characterized by pain and the lack of cooperation. Instead of working together to care for the garden, God expels them to make their own way in the wide world. Adam and Eve's biggest loss is access to the presence of God. In the garden, God walked among them. Now, they are on their own.

They pass this legacy to their children and great-grandchildren. Their son Cain kills his brother. Their great-grandson Lamech brags to his wives about taking vengeance on others. Eventually human violence is so great that God decides to hit the reset button. God sends a flood to cover the earth and start fresh with a single family. Noah is an exception to the norm. Genesis tells us that he "found favor in the eyes of the LORD" (Genesis 6:8). At his birth, Noah's father expressed his deep hope that Noah, whose name means "rest," would be able to usher in a time of rest (Genesis 5:29). Although the bar is admittedly low in his generation, Noah stands out as one who lived in harmony with God and those around him, making him the best available candidate for a new beginning. Nevertheless, the same wicked tendency to exploit rather than honor others characterizes his son Ham. Almost as soon as the flood is over, the same problems rear their ugly heads. Ham dishonors his father, introducing tension between parent and child that will send ripples through future generations.

The early chapters of Genesis culminate in a massive building project intended to make one man's empire unshakable. The builders of the tower of Babel (a.k.a. Babylon) try to lure the gods into giving their stamp of approval on the city by coming down from the heavens to dwell in it. Instead, Yahweh descends to scramble their languages and restore his vision of a multicultural world filled by humans who extend the order and fruitfulness of the garden to every place. Humans are intended to "fill the earth and subdue it," collaborating with one another to accomplish the work God delegated to us, cultivating the earth and guarding it and each other against exploitation.

It's against this backdrop of creation, failure, violence, and judgment that God chooses one man through whom he can restore his blessing to all nations—Abram. Because families and origin stories matter, Genesis begins with the story of his father, Terah.

THE FAMILY OF ABRAHAM

Emerging from the dumpster fire of rebellion, followed by the flood and tower of Babel, the author of Genesis zeroes in on one family, the family of Terah. Terah is the eighth generation after Noah's son Shem. Terah has three sons of his own, born in Ur, near Babylon: Abram, Nahor, and Haran.

Terah apparently intends to move his entire family to Canaan, but they never make it. Terah's son Haran dies in Ur. Nahor apparently stays behind when Terah packs up the rest of the family to head west. Halfway to his destination, Terah stops. Perhaps moving is more than he bargained for. Maybe business is good in the land of the Hittites. Perhaps he is tired. In any case, Terah himself settles down and eventually dies

```
Noah

Shem

SEVEN GENERATIONS

Terah

Abram   Nahor   Haran
```

Figure 1.1. Genealogy from Noah to Abram

as a resident of a place called Harran, far north of Canaan.

The name Harran is related to the Akkadian word that means "street" or "road." It's ironic, since they are en route to Canaan. The name is confusing in English, since Terah's dead son is also Haran. Does Terah name this town after his son? Not quite, since in Hebrew the town's name begins with a guttural *h*, which sounds like throat clearing, while his son's name begins with a soft *h*. Still, the similarity is unmistakable. Maybe Terah's inability to move on from Harran says something about his grief over the death of his son. He is permanently on the road. He can't let go of the past.

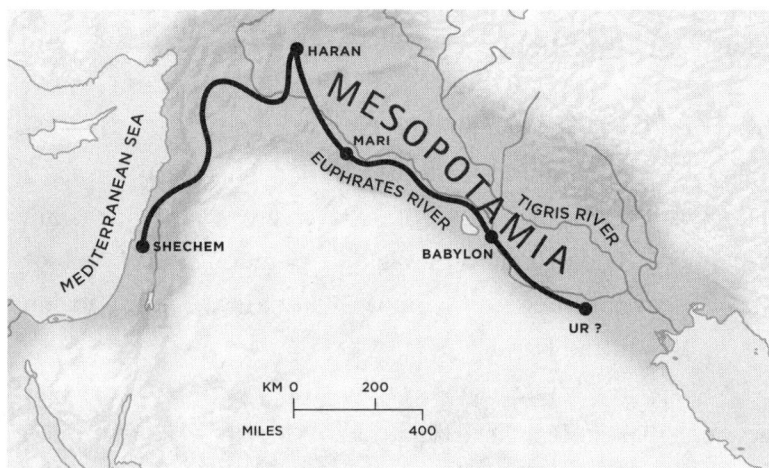

Figure 1.2. Abraham's journey from Ur to the Promised Land

After his father Terah's death, Yahweh urges Abram onward: "Go from your country, your people and your father's household to the land I will show you" (Genesis 12:1). In the ancient world, to leave one's family behind is unthinkable. Abram obeys this directive, despite its vagueness and despite how unsettling it must be to leave behind the last memories of his father and brother. Adult children were responsible to keep alive the memories of their parents and grandparents. Family members were also the first line of defense against poverty, infertility, false accusations, or mistreatment of any kind. Families were the basic building blocks of a stable society.

We might wonder whether his father Terah had instilled a love for Canaan—a place neither of them had ever seen. By leaving, Abram shows his allegiance to the God who calls to him from beyond the confines of what he knows.

Our family has moved often due to our work and schooling (sixteen times in twenty-six years of marriage, to be exact). Since our marriage, Oregon has always been home, but our children have spent very little time there. Our oldest was under two years old when we moved to the Philippines. We returned for just nine months when her younger sister was born. Our son was born in North Carolina, and our children spent their formative years there and in Illinois. It was amusing how fondly all three spoke of Oregon as the best place to live with the ideal climate. Our two younger children had never even lived there, but they spoke of Oregon as if it were the Promised Land. We moved back when they were thirteen, nine, and six. They took to Oregon like a fish takes to water. Evidently, they had inherited our love for Oregon despite not growing up there.

Had Terah spoken longingly of Canaan to Abram and his brothers? Was it the land of opportunity? We don't know what conversations unfolded around their cooking fires in Harran, but when God promises Abram great blessings, Abram does not delay. He sets out in obedience to God's voice. Although God has not specified the destination, when Abram arrives in Shechem, smack dab in the center of Canaan, God tells him: "*To your offspring* I will give this land" (Genesis 12:7).

This is one of our first clues in the Bible that God's promises are not aimed at helping us reach our personal goals. Instead, God's promises transcend our personal lives and stretch wide to encompass others we will never even meet. Abram would spend his entire life on the move, never settling down permanently. He'd go to Egypt and to Philistia, to the Negev desert and back again. As a nomad, he would keep his flocks and herds moving to find food and water. One day, many hundreds of years later, his descendants would call this land their own.

> God's promises are not aimed at helping us reach our personal goals. Instead, God's promises transcend our personal lives and stretch wide to encompass others we will never even meet.

I wonder whether our vision for our lives is too small. Whether we hope for a quiet life where we can keep our own schedule or a life as an influencer with a platform to prove it, do we ever cultivate dreams for future generations? Have you thought about your great-great-grandchildren? Or what kind of legacy you might leave behind for those who will live in your community one hundred years from now?

The author of Genesis tucks away a comment before the family leaves Ur. We might miss it if we're not paying attention: "Now Sarai was childless because she was not able to conceive" (Genesis 11:30). As Richards and James point out, in that cultural context barrenness indicated a failed marriage.[1] Essentially, Abram and his wife Sarai are stuck at the starting gate. Heartache comes in all shapes and sizes. For Sarai and Abram, it is the long wait for children with their biological clocks ticking. Abram is seventy-five years old when they pack up and head south from Harran. Still no children. Does God's promise to Abram seem like salt in the wound?

"*To your offspring* I will give this land."

That one sentence hangs in the air awkwardly, exposing their great disappointment. *Offspring? Umm . . . about that . . .*

Abram has given up on ever having children of his own, but his household is the size of a town. When Abram's nephew Lot gets into trouble later, Abram mobilizes the fighting men born in his household—all 318 of them (Genesis 14:14)! Fertility has apparently not been a problem for those minding his herds and cooking his meals, weaving his clothes and tanning his leather. Are all those pregnant bellies difficult for Sarai to see? When God appears to Abram again in a vision to reassure him, we can hear the angst in Abram's reply: "Sovereign LORD, what can you give me since I remain childless and the one who will inherit my estate is Eliezer of Damascus? . . . You have given me no children; so a servant in my household will be my heir" (Genesis 15:2-3).

At one point, a decade after their arrival in Canaan, Abram's wife, Sarai, suggests that Abram should impregnate her Egyptian maidservant. Hagar functions as a surrogate womb for Sarai. In a time before medical interventions, surrogacy of slaves was an ancient solution for infertility. However, God neither commands nor condones this behavior. The family dynamic that results is deeply problematic: Hagar despises Sarai for what she has done to her, and Sarai mistreats Hagar out of jealousy. Pregnant Hagar runs away to escape the tension, but God sends her back to Sarai for a time, probably because Hagar's chances of survival in the desert while pregnant are so low. Later, when her son is grown, Abram sends her away permanently (Genesis 16). God meets her on that journey to promise her many descendants.

In the aftermath of that messy situation, God appears to Abram again with more specific promises and instructions. Yahweh changes their names to Abraham and Sarah to symbolize a new chapter in their story. He gives them a powerful symbol of their shared commitment to living in obedience to God: circumcision.

This may seem like an odd requirement, but by marking every male in their household with a surgical sign of their covenant with Yahweh, Abraham's family experiences a daily physical reminder that God is the source of their offspring and that they must trust him for their future. God waits to bless them with a son until they have implemented the sign of the covenant because God's intentions for Abraham are much bigger than one man. They extend to all his descendants to come—even you and me. As members of the nations who would eventually find blessing through the family of Abraham, we benefit no matter our ethnic background.

Abraham's fruitfulness cannot be explained naturally. No human can take credit. Sarai's barrenness introduces a pattern that will afflict future generations as well (including Rachel, Rebekah, and Hannah). The struggle to get pregnant reminds successive generations that the gift of children is a divine blessing. Abram and Sarai are the first in God's family who must learn to wait for God to act supernaturally.

WHEN GOD'S FAMILY DOES HARM

The portrait of Abraham and Sarah in Genesis is not entirely flattering. In addition to Hagar's forced pregnancy, twice Abraham lies about his wife, Sarah, to save his own skin. This puts her in harm's way and jeopardizes the fulfillment of God's promise, while Abraham benefits handsomely. Pharaoh, king of Egypt, and Abimelech, king of Gerar, each take Sarah into his own palace with intentions to add her to the royal harem (Genesis 12; 20). When they realize she is a married woman, they both send her away with lavish gifts for Abraham, including slaves.

Speaking of slaves, Abraham and Sarah buy slaves and receive them as gifts on several occasions. This is not just a matter of ancient methods of employment. Genesis is explicit (in more ways than one) about Sarah's mistreatment of her Egyptian slave, Hagar. First, Sarah uses her to bear a child for herself. Naturally, Hagar resents being used to build someone else's family. Second, with Abraham's blessing, Sarah abuses Hagar harshly enough that Hagar runs away into the desert, where she will surely die.

The Bible does not sugarcoat the behavior of its central characters. Ironically, just as Abraham and Sarah mistreat her Egyptian slave, so the Egyptians eventually mistreat their descendants while they are enslaved in Egypt (Genesis 16:6; Exodus 1:11-12). Description is not prescription. We cannot assume that because the Bible describes something that happens, it is being held up as a positive example. In fact, the law given at Sinai prohibits such mistreatment in the strongest terms possible, as we'll see in chapter two.

God works through flawed people to accomplish his purposes. This is not to say that God ultimately tolerates harm, and neither should we. Scripture is clear that Yahweh "does not leave the guilty unpunished," which is to say that he takes sin against our fellow humans seriously (Exodus 34:7). God will ultimately bring unrepentant sin to light and punish those who committed it.

Perhaps you are among those who have been harmed by church leaders or fellow Christians. If so, please know that the way you were treated is unacceptable. God sees your suffering. He has not forgotten you and he will ultimately make things right—either in your lifetime or at the end of the age. Our capacity to hurt others and be hurt is a byproduct of God's decision to design a world in which humans have free will. We (and others) often make choices that cause harm.

Amid her mistreatment, Hagar encounters God. In their tender conversation, God speaks promises over Hagar that open a new future for her. Hagar likely feels powerless, but God empowers her to name her son, to exercise her own choice by returning home, and to hold on to his promises that her life will not become a dead end. She will have many descendants of her own. This means so much to Hagar that she becomes the first in Scripture to name God: "You are the God who sees me" (Genesis 16:13). God sees you too, and he has not forgotten your pain. Even in our pain we can walk forward in this living hope.

BIRTH OF A NEW NATION

We often think of Exodus as a liberation story about slaves set free by God. But that's a lopsided way of telling the story. Exodus is not about freedom for freedom's sake, as if it were offering a long-deserved vacation for individuals who were overworked. Exodus is the story of a change in masters. Yahweh defeats Pharaoh so that the Hebrews may go from serving Pharaoh to serving Yahweh. Repeatedly his command to Pharaoh is to "send my people away *so that they may serve me* in the desert." The Hebrews are not portrayed as a group of unfortunate individuals who happen to share the same fate. Instead, they are collectively the descendants of Abraham, Isaac, and Jacob, to whom God promised the land of Canaan.

What does it look like to serve Yahweh? Let's look at two scenes in the story that tend to get less attention. Together, these suggest that God acts to create a new nation oriented around the worship of Yahweh rather than to free individuals for a life of self-actualization. Back in Egypt, on the verge of their deliverance, God told Moses, "Tell the whole community of Israel that on the tenth day of this month each man is to take a lamb for his family, one for each household. If any household is too small for a whole lamb, they must share one with their nearest neighbor, having taken into account the number of people there are" (Exodus 12:3-4). The entire community celebrated on the same night, with every individual incorporated into a household. No one ate alone that night. Even the smallest family gathered with neighbors, enjoying the protective presence of Yahweh in their midst. The communal Passover meal initiated the formation of a new community. Pastor-theologian Mark Glanville calls this "festive kinship"—a community born out of feasting together.[2]

The second scene to notice is the song sung by the Israelites after they crossed the sea on dry ground. Having celebrated Yahweh's single-handed defeat of Pharaoh's army, the song speaks of Yahweh's guidance for "the people you have redeemed," saying, "In your strength you will guide them to your holy dwelling" (Exodus 15:13). The song culminates in this vision: "You will bring them in and plant them on the mountain of your inheritance—the place, LORD, you made for your dwelling, the sanctuary, Lord, your hands established" (Exodus 15:17). The goal of the exodus was not autonomy. The goal was a new community gathered around Yahweh's presence offering proper worship. Egypt's primary institutions were temples devoted to the worship of other gods. By leaving Egypt, the Hebrews were free to organize their society around the worship of Yahweh alone. That's what the word *service* entails in Hebrew—an act of worship. We still tip our hat to this by referring to our weekly gatherings as a worship *service*.

Yahweh calls the nation into being as they feast together, cross the sea, and enter the desert. Their initial destination is the mountain where they will experience God's presence in all its glory. The corporate singing and dancing in Exodus 15 simply cannot be replaced by individual praise. Something distinctive happens when we gather to eat and to sing the same song. Exodus 15 joins the community in a shared interpretation of the event they have just witnessed. Yahweh is the warrior who hurled Pharaoh's army into the sea.

As I point out in *Bearing God's Name*, the laws at Sinai were not
Israel's means of salvation (they were already saved!) but rather how
they would carry out their
mission *together* as God's
people. The laws are not an
individual code of conduct
but rather a collective wit-
ness to the nations. Together they entered a covenant relationship
with Yahweh. Together they would reflect God's character to a watching world. Yahweh invited them into his mission with delight, rather
than duty, by offering his own presence among them. God is not
looking for people who will do his work for him, but for those who
will carry his presence, participating *with* him.

> Something distinctive
> happens when we gather
> to eat and to sing the
> same song.

Instructions for building a tabernacle, or portable temple, domi-
nate the latter half of Exodus. We may find those chapters irrelevant,
since we have no intention of building a tabernacle today. However,
the tabernacle is essential to biblical theology because it resolves the
separation between God and humanity that resulted from Adam
and Eve's decision to disregard God's command. Their expulsion
from the garden introduced the major plot conflict of the Bible, in
search of resolution. How can humanity reunite with our Creator?
How can we experience the presence of God again?

Moses' careful attention to crafting the tabernacle according to the
divine instructions opens the way for humans to approach God's presence again. The cherubim that guarded the way to the tree of life in the
garden of Eden now mark the entrance to a portable tabernacle filled
with God's presence. Its central features, the ones that took the most
time and care to craft, were the covenant chest (or ark) and the high
priest's garments. Together they symbolized access to God's presence.

The ark was an elaborately carved chest decorated with cherubim
and carried on poles. The entire object was plated in gold, making

it the single most expensive piece of furniture in the tabernacle. The only person who had access to it was the high priest, who moved about among the people dressed in elaborate garments that reflected the glory of the most holy place and whose symbolic garments ensured every Israelite was represented by his ministry. On his chest, he wore a pouch decorated with twelve gemstones, each engraved with the name of one of the twelve tribal families.

The covenant chest looked remarkably like chests with carrying poles in Egypt that either contained idols inside or on their lids, flanked by winged protectors.[3] Parading the gods from one location to another was a regular part of Egyptian worship ceremonies. By designing the chest according to this conventional Egyptian style, Yahweh clearly communicated both his superiority over the gods of Egypt and his difference from them. The Israelites could easily see that the worship of Yahweh was meant to replace the worship of Egyptian gods, not coexist with it. While Egyptian priests carried idols of their gods on chests such as this, Yahweh could not be represented by wood or stone and could not be carried. In fact, Exodus 19:4 announces that Yahweh was the one who "carried" the Israelites to Mount Sinai. Yahweh had become the central focus of Israelite worship, replacing any so-called rivals from Egypt. The chest carried by the Israelite priests did not contain Yahweh but rather symbolized his intention to accompany them in their travels. The chest was merely his footstool (1 Chronicles 28:2).

The chest was not the only element of Israel's tabernacle that was strikingly similar to Egyptian counterparts. The dimensions of the tabernacle co-opted the layout of the war tent used by Ramesses II during the famous Battle of Kadesh. That battle was the most widely advertised battle in the ancient world.[4] Its story was carved on temple walls in at least five locations across Egypt, combining images and text, poetry and prose. Ramesses II was intensely proud of what he termed a single-handed victory over the Hittites after his troops abandoned him. The parallels between these accounts and the biblical account of Yahweh's defeat of Pharaoh at the sea are striking, but the most remarkable of all is that the dimensions of Yahweh's tabernacle mimic the dimensions of Pharaoh's war tent. Both feature a rectangular, east-facing courtyard surrounding a central rectangular reception tent whose inner chamber comprised the western third of that tent.

If the Israelites lived in Egypt during the reign of Ramesses II (which I think is likely), they could scarcely have missed the fact that Yahweh's tent followed the same model. By adopting a Pharaonic convention while subverting all its symbolism, Yahweh effectively communicated that he replaced Pharaoh as Israel's true king and that he was present among his people and fighting on their behalf. While Pharaoh slept in the inner chamber, the God of Israel could not be contained in that space (and did not sleep!). Instead, his presence was represented by the ark of the covenant and a pillar of cloud.

Moses doesn't tax the people to build such an elaborate tent. The people contribute willingly. Every tribal family participates because they all benefit from the ministry of the high priest, who has access to Yahweh's presence. Men and women contribute their wealth. Women weave the cloth needed for the curtains while men build the furniture and hammer the gold. By the end of Exodus, the tent is complete—the ultimate group project. As a community they will camp with the presence of God in their midst. They prepare for this profound new reality *together*.

Their future is not of their own making. Moses doesn't gather the tribal leaders for a brainstorming session so they can come up with a vision and mission statement or a five-year plan. The gathered community depends entirely on *Yahweh's* leadership. They await *his* presence and seek to remain faithful to *his* commands and follow *his* instructions.

What if our churches today looked more like this instead of following the latest church growth plan (which are modeled after corporate business strategies)? What if we were marked by the joy of feasting together in God's presence instead of the quest to increase "giving units" or online followers?

A MULTIETHNIC FAMILY

One feature of the Israelite community that readers often miss is how ethnically diverse it is. From the beginning, members of Jacob's family intermarry with non-Hebrews. Consider these examples from Genesis and Exodus:

- Abraham's household includes Egyptians, Canaanites, and Arameans, some of whom he acquires as gifts from Pharaoh and Abimelech, along with others who join him along the way.

- Jacob marries two women who are related to his mother, Rebekah, but by these marriages he also acquires two maidservants who are likely unrelated: Zilpah and Bilhah.[a] The children he bears by these Mesopotamian maidservants become tribal heads of Israel.

- Jacob's son Judah lives among the Canaanites, marries a Canaanite woman, and produces heirs with his daughter-in-law Tamar, who is likely a Canaanite (Genesis 38). Their descendant five generations later, Salmon, marries Rahab the Canaanite, who aids the Israelite spies and declares allegiance to Yahweh. Her son Boaz marries Ruth, the Moabite woman who demonstrates loyalty to her Israelite mother-in-law (Ruth 4). Boaz (the half-Canaanite) and Ruth (the Moabite) become the great-grandparents of king David.

- Jacob's son Joseph assimilates to Egyptian culture and marries Asenath, the daughter of an Egyptian priest (Genesis 41:45). Jacob adopts their two ethnically mixed sons, Ephraim and Manasseh, as his own (Genesis 48:5). They are counted among the twelve tribes of Israel.

- Moses, grandson of Jacob's son Levi, is raised by an Egyptian princess and marries first a Midianite woman, Zipporah, and then a Cushite woman (Exodus 2:21; Numbers 12:1). Moses maintains relations with his Midianite in-laws, relying on their advice.

- When God delivers the Israelites from Egypt, Exodus tells us that a mixed multitude joins them (Exodus 12:38). Evidently, others become convinced that Yahweh is a God they want to follow, and that this community is one they want to join.

My point is this: From the beginning, the Israelites were a multiethnic family whose most prominent members often married foreigners. Later laws against intermarriage are focused exclusively on protecting Israelite worship rather than trying to maintain the purity of the Israelite bloodline. Many Israelite laws speak of the participation of nonnatives in Israelite society. Through circumcision, the males of the family, even those of foreign blood, are eligible for full participation in the life of the community, including worship at the tabernacle.

PRESENT IN COMMUNITY

Any discussion of tabernacle worship is incomplete without a look at Leviticus. Leviticus is often described as a priestly instruction manual, but that's not quite accurate. Much of the information the priests need to do their jobs well is missing. Instead, the book addresses the people collectively regarding worship practices. They are a "kingdom of priests" and a "holy nation" (Exodus 19:5-6). Every Israelite is responsible to maintain holiness. The people benefit directly when the procedures are carried out according to God's command.

Leviticus solves a community problem introduced at the end of Exodus. They build, furnish, and consecrate the tabernacle. The awe-inspiring conclusion to this project is when the presence of God visibly takes up residence in the tabernacle, indicating that they have successfully carried out God's commands. They see God's glory manifest on top of the mountain, and with the completion of the tabernacle, the glory moves down the mountain and takes up residence among them (Exodus 40:34). God plans to live in a tent in the center of their camp. The problem is that Moses is unable to enter the tent (Exodus 40:35). This is a setback. Up until this time, Moses has communed freely with God on the mountain. He has entered the very cloud of God's presence. Now he cannot, and this loss affects the entire community because Moses is the one designated to intercede on their behalf.

What has changed? Why can Moses not enter God's presence in the tent of meeting? What is amiss? With God's presence near the whole community, the danger of ritual pollution is greater than before. The concept of ritual impurity may be foreign to modern, Western cultures, but it was widely understood in ancient times. Ritual impurity was caused by a handful of substances: bodily fluids associated with procreation, mold, mildew, skin disease, and dead bodies. To be in a state of ritual impurity was a regular part of life and was not considered sinful. However, everyone needed to know whether they were in a state of ritual purity because that determined whether it was appropriate for them to enter sacred space.

Leviticus walks the community through the necessary preparation for them to safely enter the presence of God by maintaining both ritual and moral purity. It begins with fellowship offerings in preparation for the full consecration of the priest. After the priests and the tabernacle are set apart and cleansed, the priests make offerings on behalf of the people and bless them.

The priestly blessing is a significant moment in Israel's story because the blessing confers Yahweh's name on them (Numbers 6:27), marking them as God's own people. The rest of Leviticus trains the nation regarding ritual and moral purity, festival observances, and priestly boundaries.

The global pandemic that began in 2020 provides a helpful analogy for ritual impurity. During the pandemic, our communities became more sensitive to the spread of germs. At first, no one knew exactly how Covid-19 spread and how deadly it would be, so we took various precautions to avoid contamination, including hand sanitizer, masks, and keeping our distance from one another. Getting Covid was not considered morally problematic, but entering a crowded room while sick was inappropriate because others would be put at risk of infection.

In a similar way, ritual impurity was not a moral problem unless someone who was ritually impure entered the tabernacle. Bible scholars have used the analogy of dirt to explain this.[5] In the right place, dirt is a good thing. We need soil to grow crops. Outside in the garden, dirt is fine. But a clod of dirt does not belong on your living room floor or in your bed. The ritual purity system of ancient Israel was designed to keep uncontrollable substances where they belonged. Menstrual blood and semen are both natural, God-given aspects of creation, but their unpredictability makes them too volatile for safe entrance into the tabernacle. The Bible does not explain the *reason* for the ritual purity system. It simply assumes people already understand it. Egypt and Mesopotamia had similar rules regulating sacred space, so these parameters would have seemed natural to the Israelites.

Moses charged the entire community to safeguard the divine presence in their midst by taking sacred space seriously. Just as we would not show up for a job interview with a stained shirt or to a black-tie dinner in cargo shorts, so the Israelites cannot show up to the tabernacle in a state of ritual impurity. To enter God's presence requires solemn preparation. We bear collective responsibility for it.

Leviticus is crucial in resolving the problem left hanging at the end of Exodus—Moses' inability to enter the tabernacle (Exodus 40:35). After Leviticus, the book of Numbers opens with a comment about God speaking to Moses "*in* the tent of meeting" (Numbers 1:1). Fellowship is restored, and the community is ready to move forward.

> To enter God's presence requires solemn preparation. We bear collective responsibility for it.

Numbers continues the theme of God's family. In it, we learn the layout of the Israelite camp, with all twelve tribes camped around the perimeter of the tabernacle. The people are not free to pick just any spot to pitch their tent. As Moses instructs, "The Israelites are to camp around the tent of meeting some distance from it, each of them under their standard and holding the banners of their family" (Numbers 2:2). Crossing the wilderness is not a freestyle event. The assembly is anchored around the presence of God, with designated camping spots.

We can already begin to sense how this might have implications for the church today. We no longer think about ritual purity in the same way. The death and resurrection of Christ has cleansed us once and for all. But underlying this system is something that endures. The way ancient Israel thought about worship pushes against what Myles Werntz calls "the bedrock evangelical assumption that the Christian life is ultimately an individual adventure, fundamentally between God and the soul." The ritual purity system reminds us how seriously we need to take the presence of God. It underscores the communal dimensions of worship. In these foundational books, the Bible presents the life of faith as a group project. Werntz continues, "This community is to be centered on Christ, who is present in its midst. Christ has called each person beyond themselves to be a part of this corporate body."[6] What would need to change if we took this seriously?

KEY IDEAS

- Our human vocation as God's image is to collaborate to accomplish the work God delegated to us, cultivating the earth and guarding it and each other against exploitation.

- Abraham and Sarai must learn to wait for God to provide what he promised.

- Sometimes the people of God harm others, but God sees the pain of the victims and will ultimately make things right.

- God frees the family of Abraham from slavery to become a new nation gathered around God's presence.

- The Israelites bore collective responsibility to safeguard the divine presence in their midst.

DIGGING DEEPER

Carmen Joy Imes. *Bearing God's Name: Why Sinai Still Matters.* IVP Academic, 2019.

Carmen Joy Imes. *Being God's Image: Why Creation Still Matters.* IVP Academic, 2023.

L. Michael Morales. *Exodus Old and New: A Biblical Theology of Redemption.* ESBT. IVP Academic, 2020.

Carmen Joy Imes. *Who Shall Ascend the Mountain of the Lord? A Biblical Theology of Leviticus.* NSBT. IVP Academic, 2015.

Christopher J. H. Wright. *Exodus.* Story of God. Zondervan, 2021.

Related videos from BibleProject: "Temple," "The Covenants," and "Blessing and Curse." See QR codes for these videos at the back of this book.

2

GROWING PAINS

FEASTING TOGETHER

I've suggested that we define the people of God as those who gather to wait for God to act. However, our waiting is not inactive. The laws of Deuteronomy may seem like an unlikely place to rediscover our purpose as God's people, but they begin to flesh out for us what we should get busy doing while we wait. In fact, Deuteronomy is so important in biblical theology that many scholars refer to the books that follow as the "Deuteronomistic History" (that's a mouthful!). This label recognizes that all of Israel's history is told with reference to Moses' teaching in Deuteronomy. It is the foundation for the community of faith, the anchor point to which they will return in future generations when reforms became necessary (e.g., 2 Kings 22–23).

Moses gathers the entire community for one last address before he dies. The people standing before him on the plains beside the Jordan River are the children of those who have been enslaved in Egypt. That entire generation of parents (except for Joshua and Caleb) dies in the wilderness because of their failure to trust God. Moses wants to ensure that this new generation has every resource they need to thrive in the land God promised to give them. In his sermon, Moses reminds them of God's provision through their years in the wilderness. He also rehearses the missteps of their parents to ensure they don't repeat those same mistakes. He reiterates the Ten Commandments and many other laws, all designed to ensure that as a community they embody their vocation to bear God's name among the nations.

Moses repeats the dietary restrictions that will set Israel apart as a whole. Avoiding foods that their Canaanite neighbors eat will reinforce social boundaries. He anticipates their desire for a king, giving parameters to ensure that Israel's kings do not act like those of surrounding nations. Amid all these laws, Moses instructs the community to start a collection in each village to provide emergency relief for society's most vulnerable members (Deuteronomy 14:28-29).[1] Every three years, a family is to bring a tenth of their produce. The aim is that the Levites (who don't own land), widows, orphans, and foreigners "may come and eat and be satisfied" (Deuteronomy 14:29). The term *Levites* refers to descendants from the tribe of Levi who are not from the clan of Aaron or Moses.[2] They serve the community by tending to the furnishings of the tabernacle. They depend on the support of the community so that they may devote themselves to this role. In his book *Just Discipleship*, Michael Rhodes describes this special tithe as the first known social welfare tax, a tremendous innovation in a world where kings typically taxed citizens to enrich themselves.[3]

This tax reminds me of Justo González's teaching on the Lord's Prayer in his book *Teach Us to Pray*.[4] When we pray, "Give us this day our daily bread," the request is collective, not individual. I do not just pray for God to meet *my* needs but to meet *our* needs. The prayer begins with *Our* Father, which implies that you and I are siblings in the family of faith. Sometimes God answers that prayer by providing more for you than you need to survive. Your responsibility is to share those resources with those who do not have enough, treating them like members of your own family.

People sometimes say that Christmas is for families. It's true that in the West, extended families tend to gather on Christmas. However, you might be surprised to learn that this is a relatively recent development, arising in the industrial age.[5] Historically speaking, Christmas was a time of generosity to the poor. We can recover the practices of previous generations of Christians by opening our homes to those who have nowhere else to go. Friends have opened their homes to us when we were far away from family. It's such a blessing to have a place to belong. Whether someone is lonely at the holidays or simply cannot make ends meet, according to Moses, we are all our brother's keeper. If someone is poor or isolated among us, it's our responsibility to share.

Moses' sermon in Deuteronomy puts many guardrails in place to prevent members of the community from becoming impoverished. For example, debt servitude is allowed for fellow Hebrews but limited to six years and strictly voluntary.

> If someone is poor or isolated among us, it's our responsibility to share.

Moses insists, "In the seventh year you must let them go free. And when you release them, do not send them away empty-handed. Supply them liberally from your flock, your threshing floor and your winepress. Give to them as the LORD your God has blessed you" (Deuteronomy 15:12-14).[6]

The seventh year is the year of debt cancellation for all, so no one will still have a debt to repay at that time (Deuteronomy 15:1). During the "Sabbath year," or seventh year, farmers are to leave their produce for the vulnerable, coinciding nicely with the year of release for debt slavery. This gives newly released indentured servants a buffer year so they can plant their own fields and live off their neighbors' land in the meantime. It also means landowners require less labor in the seventh year—a brilliant plan, since any indentured servants have just been released.

Speaking of tithes, even the yearly tithe benefits the community. Families are to bring a tenth of all their produce to the tabernacle, where they take part in a giant feast (Deuteronomy 14:22-27). The menu includes beef, mutton, wine, strong drink, and "anything you wish" (Deuteronomy 14:26). Rather than enriching the elite at the expense of the commoner, the tithe system reinforces community belonging for every member. Those with no land are invited to join the feast and be incorporated into the family—another example of festive kinship. All are welcome. What a radical departure from the politics of Egypt! In the kingdom of Yahweh, his intention is that everyone becomes family at Yahweh's table.

ON MISSION TOGETHER (JOSHUA)

When Israel finally crosses the Jordan and enters the land God promised to Abraham, it is a big deal. They've been waiting a long time for this moment. We might expect a feast, some dancing, a string of speeches, or at least some military exercises. What we get is a pile of rocks and a mass surgery that debilitates all the fighting men for several days. They cannot partake in the covenant benefits without first signing up for covenant membership.

The priests carrying the covenant chest lead the way in crossing the Jordan River. As soon as their feet touch the water, it stops flowing so that the people can cross on dry ground. This reenactment of the sea crossing gives this generation a taste of God's dramatic deliverance—a miracle they can hold on to when times get tough.

To help them remember the event, Yahweh tells Joshua, "Choose twelve men from among the people, one from each tribe, and tell them to take up twelve stones from the middle of the Jordan, from right where the priests are standing, and carry them over with you and put them down at the place where you stay tonight" (Joshua 4:2-3). The stones are to serve as a conversation piece, prompting the retelling of this miraculous story: "The LORD your God did to the Jordan what he had done to the Red Sea when he dried it up before us until we had crossed over. He did this so that all the peoples of the earth might know that the hand of the LORD is powerful and so that you might always fear the LORD your God" (Joshua 4:23-24).

The pile of rocks is remarkable because of where it comes from—the middle of the river floor, which recalls the miracle crossing. The pile of rocks is also important because of what it signifies—all twelve tribes cross over *together*, witnessing Yahweh's gracious provision again. The monument includes twelve stones, but it is one monument.

Next up is the circumcision of all the Israelite males with flint knives. Oddly, although the men leaving Egypt were circumcised (to celebrate the Passover; see Exodus 12), they had not circumcised their sons in the desert. This new generation needs to inscribe on their bodies the sign of the covenant. Without it, they stand outside the covenant. To remove the foreskin symbolizes leaving Egypt behind (Joshua 5:9). The sign by itself was not enough, of course. It was supposed to symbolize a heart ready to obey God (Deuteronomy 10:16). The prophets would later chastise the people for assuming that the physical sign of circumcision was sufficient on its own, without a change of heart (Jeremiah 4:4).

Ancient Israelites did not practice female circumcision, but a woman was included in the covenant with Yahweh through her relationship to her father, husband, and sons, all of whom were circumcised. This might not be fully appreciated in modern cultures that emphasize personal autonomy, but when community is the most important factor in determining someone's identity, then belonging is the highest value. Every woman belongs by virtue of her place in the family.

So, the first order of business in Canaan is circumcision of all the males. Then they are ready to take possession of the land. After the initial battles against Jericho and Ai, Joshua builds an altar on Mount Ebal to renew the covenant (Joshua 8:30-32). It's not that the covenant is in disrepair. Covenant renewal is essential because they have finally arrived in the land. Land possession is a benefit of covenant membership. Since all the males are circumcised, they all qualify for covenant membership. Notice that *everyone* is present—"all the Israelites, with their elders, officials and judges. . . . Both the foreigners living among them and the native-born were there" (Joshua 8:33). The narrator circles back again to affirm, "There was not a word of all that Moses had commanded that Joshua did not read to the whole assembly of Israel, including the women and children, and the foreigners who lived among them" (Joshua 8:35).

I wonder sometimes whether we've lost our vision for gatherings of this magnitude. We so often segregate into children's programs, youth groups, young adults, young marrieds, empty nesters, or retirees. Women gather. Men gather. Singles gather. When do we *all* gather? What do we miss if we don't?

The faith we share transcends age, gender, and citizenship. Before we had children, my husband and I were insistent that families should worship together. Why whisk the children away to Sunday school when they could be formed from childhood as a participant in the larger body of Christ? As I mentioned, that was *before* we had kids. After our oldest was born, we realized this was not as easy as we thought. Colic made it impossible for both of us to be in the service with our daughter.

> When do we *all* gather?
> What do we miss if we don't?

Along the way, we've seen some wonderful examples of family worship. The first was in our chapels at Prairie College. Each semester, our college president, Mark Maxwell, would stand up front, usually holding his granddaughter, to make an important announcement to the effect of, "I want you to know that children are welcome here. You might hear the chatter of little voices, some crying or whining during chapel, and you might see some wiggles. Please don't let this bother you. Every child in this room signifies a parent who can participate. We are glad to have them here." I love the way Mark set the tone for our school culture as one that welcomed children the way Jesus did.

Our current church in California includes children at the beginning and end of the service. Children of all ages join us for the welcome, announcements, the prayer of intention, and singing the Lord's Prayer. Before the sermon, the children come up to the front so that we can pray a blessing over them: "Beloved children, may the Lord bless you as you hear his Word. May you remember all the wonderful things he's done for you. And when you return, we will celebrate God's work together. The Lord be with you!" To which all the children respond with enthusiasm, "And also with you!"

Before Communion, the children return so they can participate by receiving a blessing at the Communion table. Families come forward together as we corporately participate in the Lord's supper. An adult stands at either side of the Communion table to pray a blessing over the children, so that even if they are not yet ready to partake, they are welcomed.

The positive nature of Israel's corporate celebrations for all ages are just one side of the coin. Israel celebrates together, but when they tolerate covenant unfaithfulness in their midst, they also suffer the consequences together. We'll explore their collective failures after we address another urgent question: What about the Canaanites?

CANAANITE GENOCIDE?

One of the most pressing questions people today raise about the Old Testament concerns the so-called Canaanite genocide. How could God tell his people to kill so many innocent people? This is a difficult question that requires a whole book to address all the angles. Here I want to highlight just two neglected approaches to this question.

1. Read Yahweh's instructions more carefully. Sometimes our summaries of the so-called conquest lack precision. On three occasions, Moses instructed the people regarding their entrance into Canaan: Exodus 23:20-33; Deuteronomy 7:1-6; and Deuteronomy 12:1-3. A close reading of all three passages shows that the primary focus of the conquest was to destroy the means for worship of false gods. They were to smash *idols and altars*, not people. They were to chisel out the names *of foreign gods* so they could establish the worship of Yahweh instead. In other words, although Canaanites died when they resisted Israel's army, killing them was not the focus of Yahweh's instructions. Israel's primary purpose was to dismantle false worship. God's plan was to drive the people out ahead of the Israelite invasion.

Matthew Lynch points out in his book *Flood and Fury* that when the Israelite troops first arrive in Canaan, they use their weapons on themselves to perform circumcision. The Canaanites are *herem*, or "off-limits," for the Israelites, who cannot make covenants with them or intermarry with them or take them as slaves. That our English translations render *herem* as "destroy totally" obscures the fact that anything *herem* is subject to "irrevocable surrender to God."[a] Do people die? Yes, but many flee before the Israelites arrive, and others surrender, as we will see next.

2. Recognize the collectivist values of these cultures. What bothers us today about the conquest did not embarrass the biblical authors. They understood that the people of Canaan were—for the most part—a package deal. Kinship connected every member of society into a strong web of relations centered on the worship of false gods.

Our concern about innocent individuals would have struck ancient Israelites as odd. These societies were cohesive units in which each person's identity was bound up with their neighbors. Together they worshiped Baal and Asherah. The prophet Jeremiah describes false worship as a family affair: "The children gather wood, the fathers light the fire, and the women knead the dough and make cakes to offer to the Queen of Heaven. They pour out drink offerings to other gods to arouse my anger" (Jeremiah 7:18). Even children participated in the worship of false gods. Their parents trained them from infancy in the community's values.

That's what makes the behavior of Rahab the Canaanite even more remarkable. She shows disloyalty to her king, her people, and the gods of Canaan when she declares allegiance to Yahweh and aids the spies in their escape from Jericho. Her inclusion in the people of God shows us there is no middle ground—either one is for Yahweh or against him. Canaan has no innocent bystanders. Either the Canaanites must leave, or they must join Israel as covenant members who worship Yahweh. Rahab demonstrates that any Canaanite can enter the people of God if they follow her example.

This important question cannot be fully answered in a page or two, and it may be impossible to reach full clarity on why God chose this unrepeatable and targeted method of establishing his kingdom. Our cultural distance from ancient Israel makes it difficult to appreciate what God is doing.

See the "Digging Deeper" section at the end of this chapter for resources that address this issue more comprehensively.

COLLECTIVE FAILURE

Yahweh's vision for a covenant community centered on the divine presence comes unraveled in the book of Judges. The deaths of Joshua and the elders of Israel mark the end of an era of covenant faithfulness (Joshua 24:31; Judges 2:7). The tribes of Israel disperse, with no central leadership and little memory of what Yahweh has done for them (Judges 2:10). God raises up a series of judges to decide court cases or discern what is best for the community and lead the people in battle.

After the first few decent judges—Othniel, Ehud, Shamgar, and Deborah—the rest are complicated figures, each one more problematic than the last. Deborah is the highwater mark, not only leading successfully in battle and judging court cases but also serving as a prophet. After her, we read about Gideon the coward and idolater, Abimelech and Jephthah, both problematic militia leaders, and Samson, an incredibly strong man driven by his lust. Truly none of these belongs in a book of Bible heroes. The point of the book is Israel's gradual and cyclical apostasy.

The book of Judges closes with two brutal stories to illustrate the depths to which Israel had fallen. Everything goes wrong in these stories. Believe me when I say this is going to turn your stomach. In the first, a Levite (who should be serving Yahweh in the tabernacle) wanders off and agrees to serve as a priest-for-hire in the household shrine of a thief and idol worshiper (Judges 17). When a better offer comes along—serving the whole tribe of Danites as priest instead—he abandons his previous commitment and goes with the renegade tribe on their mission to slaughter unsuspecting neighbors and take land God had not allotted to them (Judges 18). We don't find out until the end of this story that the Levite is none other than the grandson of Moses (Judges 18:30). That signals that the stories of Judges do not appear chronologically.

Truly, this story is a testament to how quickly and thoroughly things can go awry when faith is not passed from one generation to the next. Reading this tale of blatant disregard for Yahweh's teachings prepares us for the next story, the most brutal of its kind in the entire Bible. The matter-of-fact nature of its telling has led some of my students to assume that God was not troubled by the egregious violence against women in this story. On the contrary, by beginning with the story of the rebel Levite, the author of Judges has prepared us to see this story as a complete collapse of Israelite standards. God's people have become indistinguishable from the Canaanites.

The refrain of these chapters offers subtle commentary: "In those days Israel had no king" (Judges 18:1; 19:1). The implication is finally stated at the close of the book: "In those days Israel had no king; everyone did as they saw fit" (Judges 21:25). Presumably, a king could have kept the nation from going off the rails by providing national identity and cohesion. But they had no king. To judge by their behavior, not even God was their king. So, when the story of the Levite and his concubine opens in Judges 19, we need to carry with us an accurate set of expectations. Anything goes in this dumpster fire of an era.

The narrator doesn't tell us whether this is the same Levite we met earlier in chapter 17. Maybe, maybe not. They live in the same area— the hill country of Ephraim. They both have connections in Bethlehem. This Levite has a concubine, a wife of unequal social status, who leaves him and returns home to her father in Bethlehem. The Levite goes to retrieve her four months later, enjoys his father-in-law's generous hospitality for a few days, and then takes his servant and his concubine and sets out for home.

In that cultural context, hospitality is the cardinal virtue. Ancient Israel has no motels. Travelers depend on the generosity of locals who take them in for the night. The narrator's elaborate recounting of the hospitality of his host in Bethlehem sets us up to watch whether others will follow suit. On the way home, the Levite's servant suggests that they stop for the night in Jebus. The Levite refuses because, although later it would become the Israelite capital of Jerusalem, at this time, Jebus is not an Israelite city. He implies that it would not be safe to stay there. Instead, they go on to Gibeah, a town occupied by the tribe of Benjamin.

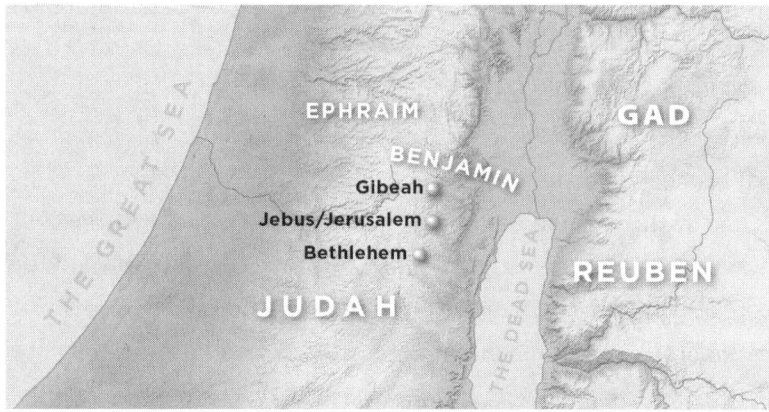

Figure 2.1. Map of the hill country

No Benjamite family takes them in for the night (a serious breach of hospitality standards). However, a man from the tribe of Ephraim lives in that city and offers them food and shelter. We don't expect the story to proceed without incident, but it is still shocking when the men of Gibeah pound on the door of the house, demanding that the host turn over the Levite so they can get to know him (Judges 19:22). Their intentions to rape him are obvious. The echoes of the story of Sodom and Gomorrah from Genesis 19 are unmistakable.

This is the extreme opposite of hospitality, and the host calls it what it is: "vile" and "outrageous" (Judges 19:23). By taking the man in for the night, the host has pledged protection, so he refuses their wicked request. But what happens next is truly nauseating: the host offers his own daughter and the Levite's concubine to satisfy the men's appetites for sexual violence, saying, "You can use them and do to them whatever you wish" (Judges 19:24). This is misogyny, plain and simple. The host values men over women. Any society where women are not safe—where their voices are not heard and their lives are not valued—is a society completely out of alignment with God's will.

The story ends badly. The men of Gibeah rape and abuse the Levite's concubine all night long, leaving her for dead. Her husband gets up in the morning, finds her at the threshold of the house, and callously says, "Get up; let's go." When she doesn't answer, he slings her over his donkey and heads home. While he takes

> Any society where women are not safe—where their voices are not heard and their lives are not valued—is a society completely out of alignment with God's will.

no responsibility for her plight and shows her no shred of compassion, he apparently feels his own honor has been violated. He decides the nation needs a wakeup call, so wake them up he does.

Taking a knife, he cuts his concubine into twelve pieces, sending her dismembered body throughout the land of Israel. The chapter concludes, "Everyone who saw it was saying to one another, 'Such a thing has never been seen or done, not since the day the Israelites came up out of Egypt. Just imagine! We must do something! So speak up!'" (Judges 19:30).

In response to this wakeup call, eleven tribes assemble and determine to bring justice to Gibeah. They notify the tribe of Benjamin about the crime that has occurred, calling them to hand over the perpetrators "so that we may put them to death and purge the evil from Israel" (Judges 20:13). Tragically, the men of Benjamin refuse. Instead, they double down and rally for war. They prefer to fight their fellow Israelites to the death rather than hold their brothers accountable for their sin. This reveals everything we need to know about how far they have fallen. Any community that attempts to shield perpetrators instead of their victims is inviting God to bring judgment. Again, the narrator reveals a key time marker near the end of the story: "The ark of the covenant of God was there, with Phinehas the son of Eleazar the son of Aaron, ministering before it" (Judges 20:27-28). That situates this story just three generations after leaving Egypt.[7] When Israel entered Canaan, Eleazar was high priest. Now his son has taken over, likely just a couple of decades since their arrival in the land.

The Israelites have already lost their way. Covenant faithfulness has given way to rape culture. Rather than protecting the vulnerable, they exploit them. By siding with the perpetrators, the men of Benjamin put themselves in the crosshairs of God's judgment and at odds with their fellow Israelites.

#CHURCHTOO

Stories like this one play out far too often today, even in churches. Church and denominational leaders are sometimes more committed to protecting their buddies from the consequences of sinful actions than they are committed to cultivating a culture of safety and justice. The results are devastating to anyone who has been abused. Abuse that takes place in church is already deeply devastating to survivors because the place where people are supposed to receive spiritual care becomes a nightmare of harm instead. When a church or Christian organization refuses to listen to survivors or to advocate on their behalf, the impact of that harm is multiplied. Survivors can no longer tell themselves that what they experienced was one bad apple. Instead, they discover a whole system in place to protect bad apples.

The New Testament says that teachers are held to a higher standard of accountability (James 3:1) and that those who harm little ones are in special danger of judgment (Luke 17:2; see also Exodus 22:22-24). We cannot side with sin and expect God's Spirit to move unhindered in our communities.

At Sinai, when Moses passes on God's instructions for the Israelite community, he reserves his strongest words for cases like this. As we discussed earlier, the point of the laws is to shape Israelite society, helping them to reflect God's character to their neighbors. Of all the laws I've seen in the Bible, none carries more weight than this one: "Do not mistreat or oppress a foreigner, for you were foreigners in Egypt. Do not take advantage of the widow or the fatherless. If you do and they cry out to me, I will certainly hear their cry" (Exodus 22:21-23).

Exodus 22:22 is especially poignant in Hebrew, which has a distinctive way of placing emphasis by doubling the verb. Here's my wooden translation: "If you oppress-oppress them, so that they cry-out-cry-out to me, I will hear-hear their cry." Doubling is one way to make something emphatic in Hebrew: "If you in fact oppress them, so that they cry out emphatically to me, then I will certainly hear their cry."

I have not found another law in Exodus with triple emphasis like this one. And God shows he is serious by imposing a severe penalty: "My anger will be aroused, and I will kill you with the sword; your wives will become widows and your children fatherless" (Exodus 22:24). The punishment fits the crime. If you take advantage of those without male protectors, then your own family will lack male protectors. It's another way of stating the golden rule of God's judgment found in the book of the prophet Obadiah: "As you have done, it will be done to you; your deeds will return upon your own head" (Obad 15).

When our communities are marked by care for the most vulnerable, then we need not fear becoming vulnerable ourselves. On judgment day, let us be found among those who refuse to tolerate the presence of exploitation among us. May we never respond to abuse with a nonchalant "Mistakes happen." Instead, may we take seriously the charge to look out for others. No human being is worthy of mistreatment.

FAMILY LOYALTY

The beautiful story of Ruth is even more remarkable against the backdrop of the book of Judges. The gruesome story we've just encountered reminds us that Ruth was in grave danger when she returned to Bethlehem with Naomi, whose husband, Elimelech, and both of her sons had died. If even married women were vulnerable in the days of the Judges, imagine the plight of a woman with no husband, no father, and no son to protect her.

In a world where kinship means everything, Ruth's decision to stick with Naomi is remarkable. Naomi has no family tree to offer shelter to Ruth. That leaves Ruth almost no hope of remarriage. Ruth is a Moabite, the historic enemy of Israel. Without a husband, Ruth will not have children. Without children, she will have no one to care for her in her old age. Still, Ruth insists on accompanying Naomi back to Bethlehem to provide for Naomi's needs. She understands that this entails a radical change in loyalties. She leaves behind her family and country of origin. As such, her declaration is a model of what it means to become part of God's family: "Don't urge me to leave you or to turn back from you. Where you go I will go, and where you stay I will stay. Your people will be my people and your God my God. Where you die I will die, and there I will be buried. May the LORD deal with me, be it ever so severely, if even death separates you and me" (Ruth 1:16-17). Ruth's vision of family loyalty extends even into death. To become part of Naomi's family means accepting the fate of her family line, even if it is snuffed out.

We see a similar commitment from Joseph in Genesis. While separated from his family, he rises to the top leadership position in Egypt by Pharaoh's side. When his birth family is forced to go to Egypt to find food to survive the famine, Joseph has a choice. He can maintain ties with royalty in Egypt. He has married well. No doubt he has great wealth. But before Joseph dies, he gives urgent instructions to his brothers, trusting them to pass them on to their children. These instructions tell us where his true loyalties are: "And Joseph made the Israelites swear an oath and said, 'God will surely come to your aid, and *then you must carry my bones up from this place*'" (Genesis 50:25).

While Joseph's sense of family loyalty is questionable in his younger years, his reunification with his brothers in Egypt proves transformative. All the success of Egypt cannot outweigh Joseph's fundamental sense of identity rooted in his heritage. Joseph's ultimate hope is in Yahweh's promises to Abraham to give him the land of Canaan. Even his bones belong there.

Perhaps one reason the new pharaoh of Exodus does not know Joseph (Exodus 1:6, 8) is that he has no tomb in Egypt. His hope is not in the afterlife as the Egyptians conceive of it. In contrast, Joseph is well-remembered by the Israelites. His sons Ephraim and Manasseh become tribal heads, accounting for a major share of the land of Canaan.

Ruth, too, fares better than expected. In Bethlehem she demonstrates her loyalty to Naomi by gleaning (picking up leftover stalks of grain) in the fields. The man in whose field she works turns out to be a relative of her dead father-in-law, a distant branch on the family tree. Boaz recognizes Ruth's admirable commitment to Naomi's well-being and responds favorably to her request that he redeem their family by marrying her.

Ruth's appeal is based on an ancient practice known as levirate marriage, in which a *levir* (or brother-in-law) agrees to carry on a childless brother's family line by marrying his widow. Their offspring inherit the land or wealth that normally would have belonged to the dead brother. It is a selfless act because if a man dies without offspring, his surviving brothers stand to gain a greater share of the inheritance. Those willing to perform this service receive public honor, while those who refuse are shamed.

Levirate marriage points to the importance of belonging. It keeps the land in the family, carries on the name of the deceased, and maintains continuity for the bereaved woman as part of the community. The book of Ruth shows us that the general principles of levirate marriage could be extended to include even a foreigner who had joined the people of Israel. Although Boaz is a more distant relative, he takes responsibility for the redemption of both the land and family tree of Elimelech.

Without Ruth's selfless ingenuity and Boaz's generosity, the line of David (and eventually the Messiah, Jesus) would have been snuffed out. Both act for the sake of the greater good. Integrity sometimes demands that we work against our own self-interest.

In a way, the stories of Ruth and Joseph are complementary. Ruth begins as a foreigner but becomes a member of God's covenant family. Joseph begins as a member of the covenant family, becomes estranged, and nearly assimilates to a foreign context, but then reaffirms his core identity as a descendant of Abraham. Both indicate their intention to be buried alongside their true family. Now that's commitment.

> Integrity sometimes demands that we work against our own self-interest.

In the early centuries of the church, believers met for worship near the graves of church members in the catacombs. Later, when churches began to own property, Christians began burying their dead in the churchyard or even under the sanctuary floor. Like

Joseph's, this burial practice made permanent their sense of belonging to the family of faith.

With all these stories, we see how a shared commitment to Yahweh's mission brought unlikely people together as participants in God's family. And so it is with God's family today. By living out a commitment to God, we become family with one another.

Who are your people? Where do your bones belong? Can you imagine giving up your own future to care for someone who is otherwise vulnerable? Have you seen anyone do that in modern times? Mother Teresa devoted her life to serving those from the lowest caste in India, the Dalits, by offering them a way to die with dignity. Those she served would never be able to offer her public honor or bequeath wealth to her. They had none. She emptied herself for their sakes, to show them they were worthy of love as men and women created by God. She left her home in Albania to live among them in Calcutta' until her own death in 1997, when she was buried in the Mother House of the Missionaries of Charity in Calcutta. Her loyalty and commitment to the Indian people were truly remarkable. We can follow her example by cultivating ties with people outside our natural family and demonstrating deep and abiding solidarity with them.

KEY IDEAS

- All those who feast together at Yahweh's table become family.
- Circumcision was the prerequisite for corporate worship gatherings because it signified collective commitment to Yahweh.
- Israel quickly forgot Yahweh and what he had done for them, spiraling downward and becoming a community that tolerated idolatry and abuse. God takes abuse very seriously, judging those who allow it in their communities.
- A shared commitment to Yahweh's mission brings unlikely people together as participants in God's family.

DIGGING DEEPER

Paul Copan. *Is God a Moral Monster? Making Sense of the Old Testament God.* Baker, 2011.

Matthew J. Lynch. *Flood and Fury: Old Testament Violence and the Shalom of God.* IVP Academic, 2023.

Michael J. Rhodes. *Just Discipleship: Biblical Justice in an Unjust World.* IVP Academic, 2023.

Charlie Trimm. *The Destruction of the Canaanites: God, Genocide, and Biblical Interpretation.* Eerdmans, 2022.

Christopher Wright. *The God I Don't Understand: Reflections on Tough Questions of Faith.* Zondervan, 2016.

Related videos from BibleProject: "Joshua," "Judges," and "Ruth."

3

FAMILY DYSFUNCTION

MESSY FAMILIES

By now you've noticed that this book is not like a bag of microwave popcorn, offering a quick and easy snack. It's more like a roast that spends all day in the smoker. As we patiently trace what the Bible has to say about the faith community, we develop more robust sensibilities about how to think about the church. Can our background disqualify us from membership in God's family? How should we respond when the church harms people? What is our responsibility for the sins of our ancestors? The answers to these questions are hiding in plain sight if we take the time to read Scripture more carefully.

The first three chapters of 1 Samuel zero in on a family from the "hill country of Ephraim." Given the torturous tales that end the book of Judges involving people from the hill country of Ephraim, our expectations are low. We wonder whether any faithful followers of Yahweh are left who gather to worship and wait for God to intervene. We meet a woman named Hannah, whose family situation is challenging, to put it mildly. Her husband has taken a second wife, perhaps because she is barren. Although her husband still loves and provides for her, Hannah's co-wife torments her over her barrenness. The dysfunction of her family and the grief of childlessness both weigh heavily on her.

Hannah encounters Eli at a point of desperation when she is pouring out her heart to the Lord in prayer. Eli is serving as priest at the tabernacle in Shiloh, and Hannah's family has come there to worship. Eli assumes her emotional display is due to drunkenness, which tells us that worship in his day was more likely to be characterized by excess wine than sincere prayer. However, Hannah's genuine prayer and her family's regular trips to the tabernacle to worship set them apart in their generation as people devoted to Yahweh. They were among the faithful who gathered to wait for God to fulfill his promises. When Hannah speaks to Eli about her deep "anguish and grief," he pronounces a blessing over her: "Go in peace, and may the God of Israel grant you what you have asked of him" (1 Samuel 1:16-17).

Yahweh does just that—he intervenes supernaturally in answer to her prayers. He has mercy on Hannah and grants her a son, whom she names Samuel, which means "God has heard." After she weans him at three years old, Hannah brings Samuel to the tabernacle, declaring to Eli: "I prayed for this child, and the LORD has granted me what I asked of him. So now I give him to the LORD. For his whole life he will be given over to the LORD" (1 Samuel 1:27-28).

The story of Hannah's son, Samuel, appears side by side with the story of Eli's sons, with the narrator switching back and forth scene by scene between them to highlight the contrast. Eli's family is severely dysfunctional. His sons are complete scoundrels, disregarding the Levitical instructions on proper sacrifice and using their position to take advantage of others. Samuel, on the other hand, faithfully serves Yahweh. The narrator tells us, "And the boy Samuel continued to grow in stature and in favor with the LORD and with people" (1 Samuel 2:26).

Technically, Samuel should not be a priest, because he is not from the tribe of Levi. The narrator introduces the family as Ephraimites, having descended from Joseph. However, Hannah dedicated Samuel to Yahweh for temple service.

Simultaneously, a prophet announces to Eli that his own family will be cut off from temple service because of their rebellion. Yahweh says, "I will raise up for myself a faithful priest, who will do according to what is in my heart and mind. I will firmly establish his priestly house, and they will minister before my anointed one always" (1 Samuel 2:35). That faithful priest is obviously Samuel, who also receives a prophetic word from Yahweh regarding the house of Eli. By the end of 1 Samuel 3, all Israel knows that Samuel is a prophet of Yahweh, serving in the tabernacle at Shiloh. Sometimes God's way of intervening is to color outside the lines.

Perhaps this is why the Chronicler feels justified in grafting Samuel into the family tree of Levi. If you're like most people, you skim over the genealogies or skip them altogether. But when we do that, we miss out on some of the most intriguing clues to a book's theological priorities.

First Chronicles 6:16-28 records the descendants of Levi. For the most part, the genealogy is linear rather than segmented. We don't get *all* the sons of each generation but only a particular family line that leads down to the present community. Levi has three sons, each of whom have multiple sons, but the family line of only grandson from each son is traced: Gerson's son Libni, Kohath's grandson Korah, and Merari's son Mahli. Oddly, the lineage of Samuel's ancestor, Elkanah, appears with no warning in this section on Levi, without clarifying how it fits into the family of Levi or Korah (1 Chronicles 6:25-30).[1] The Chronicler introduces Elkanah as if he's a grandson of Levi, but he's not.

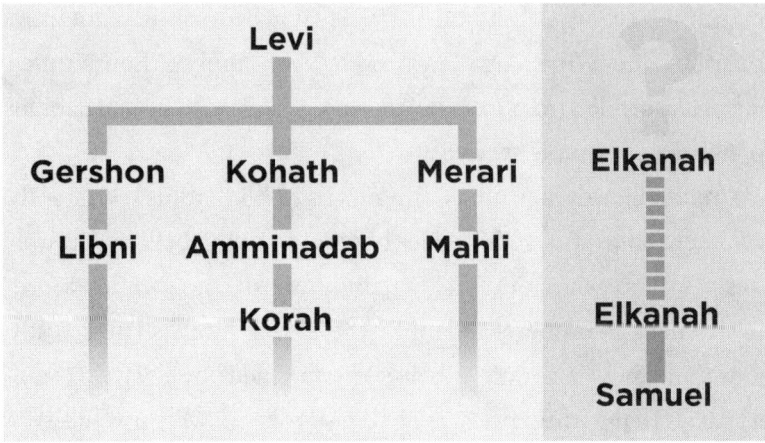

Figure 3.1. The descendants of Levi

What seems evident is that the Chronicler has theological reasons for including Samuel in the family of Levi. To identify him as a Levite justifies Samuel's career trajectory as a priest. Samuel serves as prophet, judge, and priest—the latter without legal qualifications but with demonstrable qualifications of character and faithfulness. God replaces Eli's sons, removing them from the priesthood and selecting Samuel instead. The virtual adoption of Samuel by a priest makes it natural to include him. Strikingly, the family of Eli is nowhere to be seen in the Chronicler's genealogy.

The idea that Samuel became a priest without the right pedigree encourages me. It tells me that God is not limited by our family line. He raises up who he wills. In this case, God redeems one family mess (Eli's) by working in another messy family (Hannah's) to bring about something entirely new. One faithful follower of Yahweh makes all the difference.

I grew up in a family that from the outside looked postcard-worthy. Each passing decade shows me more of the truth about how messy things really were. Alongside many positive qualities such as hard work and faithful service and resourcefulness and generosity, our family was plagued by hidden addictions, adultery, abuse, divorce, grudges, narcissism, and gaslighting. My grandparents frequently bragged that all their children and grandchildren were following Jesus. That was a misleading generalization. Under the pretty carpet there was rot in the floorboards.

> God is not limited by our family line. He raises up who he wills.

Thankfully, dysfunctional families cannot derail God's wider purposes. While unfaithfulness puts us outside God's blessing, coming from messy families does not in itself make us ineligible. Instead, God can draft us onto his winning team—his covenant family.

FOOD (IN)SECURITY

If the idea that God redeems messy family situations gets you excited, you are not alone. When Hannah brings her three-year-old son, Samuel, back to the tabernacle to dedicate him to Yahweh's service, she can hardly contain herself. The overflow of her heart is a prophetic prayer. Like a musical that conveys its most important messages in song, so the book of 1 Samuel conveys its richest theology in poetry. Hannah's prayer in 1 Samuel 2 offers a preview of the central dynamics of the entire book, while David's song and his poetic final words in 1 Samuel 22–23 summarize the great things Yahweh accomplished.

One aspect of Hannah's prayer is especially relevant to the theme of God's covenant family. Hannah prays about food, recognizing that providing food for others is a key marker of faithfulness to God. As Old Testament scholar Denise Flanders explains, "In the ancient Near East, the royal ability to control and redistribute food served to create and maintain political power; the book of Samuel suggests that such capability need be governed by [Yahweh's] commitment to provide food for all."[2]

The issue of food begins with Hannah herself. Although her husband gives her a double portion of meat, it seems small in comparison to her co-wife Peninnah, who receives a portion for each of her children as well (1 Samuel 1:4-5).[3] Peninnah's mocking makes it impossible for Hannah to eat at all. When she returns several years later with her son, Samuel, God's answer to her prayers, she brings her own food to sacrifice—a bull, flour, and wine (1 Samuel 1:24).

Hannah's prayer reflects this reversal. She prays, "Those who were full hire themselves out for food, but those who were hungry are hungry no more. She who was barren has borne seven children, but she who has had many sons pines away" (1 Samuel 2:5). Hannah's words are not just personal. After all, she has only one son, not seven. Her prayer reflects broader truths about the way God works. Eli's sons, who had wrongly fattened themselves on the offerings of the people, will be cut off so that their descendants will have to beg for food (1 Samuel 2:36). As Flanders explains, Yahweh "condemns disparities in which the rich are indulgent and the poor lack food."[4]

The theme of food distribution continues throughout the books of Samuel. As an adult, Samuel anoints the first two kings of Israel at feasts (1 Samuel 9:19-24; 16:1-13). King Saul's folly is demonstrated in part by the oath he takes that prevents his fighting men from eating anything (1 Samuel 14:24), while David brings food for the soldiers and their commander even before he is king (1 Samuel 17:17).

David feeds the hungry and restores stolen property. On his most important feast day, he ensures that every person present receives an equal portion of food: "a loaf of bread, a cake of dates and a cake of raisins to each" (2 Samuel 6:19).[5] Toward the end of his reign, David experiences the consequences of his own covenant unfaithfulness. He finds himself on the run from his son Absalom and in need of sustenance. As he experiences the downside of reversed fortunes, two men meet him in the wilderness and provide food: Ziba and

Barzillai (2 Samuel 16:2; 17:27-28). By providing for David and his men, they participate in the restoration of his kingship.

In Flanders's words,

> Hannah's song and story laid out a vision with respect to food. It operates from the conviction that in God's economy, everyone has enough to eat (Genesis 1:29; Psalm 104:27; 145:15). The song declares that when there are imbalances, God rights them by feeding the hungry and replacing the indulgence of the overfed with hunger (1 Samuel 2:5). [Yahweh's] anointed king should embrace these same values—first ensuring that everyone has enough, and then when an imbalance occurs, righting those wrongs.[6]

Have you experienced food insecurity? This term describes the experience of not knowing where your next meal will come from. A surprising number of US residents live with ongoing food insecurity. This is one factor that has prompted many to advocate for free school lunches. Children cannot be expected to focus during class when they are hungry.

Our family went through a season of financial hardship when I was in junior high. My dad lost his closet-shelving business in part because of a housing crash that halted new construction. We learned to scrimp and save wherever possible, wearing hand-me-down clothes and reusing everything. My mom cringed every time the phone rang because creditors kept calling. The IRS seized my dad's truck and copy machine—the only items of real value we had, and precisely the items he needed most to be able to keep working. (My dad's dad bailed us out of this predicament by buying the truck and copy machine back from the IRS for us.) For about a year, we got most of our food from a local food pantry. I never personally worried about having enough to eat because my mom was the one who bore that burden. We ate a lot of macaroni and cheese with canned tuna, peanut butter sandwiches, and Spam with canned peaches on rice (which is not a bad combination, actually).

I don't worry about food anymore. I think less about price tags than I ever have. However, according to Hannah's song, I'm in a more dangerous position. Having plenty can make it easy to forget what it was like to have to choose between food and education or between food and clothes or between food and rent. Hannah's song reminds me that God has never stopped thinking about this. God's desire is that everyone has enough. The abundance we enjoy is God's invitation to us to partner with him to ensure that everyone has what they need.

ADVENTURES IN MISSING THE POINT

With apologies to *Veggie Tales*, the story of David and Goliath is *not* meant to reassure us that "little guys can do big things too." It's such a well-known story and is so often told to children that an oversimplified version of it lives in our heads and obscures the point. As we explored in the previous section, Hannah's song sets the trajectory for the whole book of 1 Samuel by highlighting divine reversals. "The bows of the warriors are broken, but those who stumbled are armed with strength" (1 Samuel 2:4). The song ends with a resounding claim that seems to anticipate David's victory over the giant: "It is not by strength that one prevails; those who oppose the LORD will be broken. The Most High will thunder from heaven; the LORD will judge the ends of the earth. He will give strength to his king and exalt the horn of his anointed" (1 Samuel 2:9-10). Goliath is certainly strong, but he opposes Yahweh, so he is brought down to the grave. Reflecting on Hannah's song, a reader of Samuel might wonder which king God will supply with strength.

The entire plot of the book of 1 Samuel highlights the downward slide of King Saul and David's rise to power, mirroring the reversals in Hannah's song. The author of 1 Samuel aims to demonstrate that David is the rightful king, chosen by God. Saul has three strikes against him (see 1 Samuel 13, 14, and 15), followed by Samuel's anointing of David as a replacement king (1 Samuel 16). The story of David and Goliath comes in the awkward period between David's anointing and his accession to the throne. Saul is still king. His paranoia fuels his obsession to stamp out anyone he feels is a threat to his kingship, which is usually David.

If you're from an individualist culture, like I am, Goliath's challenge might be misleading. Yes, he's tall and strong and ready to pound whoever fights him, but the battle is not actually a showdown between two individuals. They are simply tokens who represent their respective communities and their gods. In the ancient Near East, every battle was considered divine warfare. Every army commander relied on his god to bring victory. Whoever won this battle would prove the superiority of their god and (accordingly) their king.

Day after day, Goliath challenges the Israelite army to send a man to fight him in a contest. The narrator is clear: "Saul and all the Israelites were dismayed and terrified" (1 Samuel 17:11). But should they be? If this is Yahweh's battle, it matters little who they send. They are intimidated by what their eyes can see instead of relying on God to act on their behalf.

We all know Goliath was tall. In Hebrew, he was "six cubits and a span" (1 Samuel 17:4). A cubit is the distance from elbow to fingertip (about eighteen inches), while a span is the distance between the tip of the thumb and the tip of a little finger with fingers spread wide (about six inches). That would make Goliath about 9.5 feet tall. However, the Greek translation of the Old Testament has Goliath instead at "four cubits and a span," which works out to about 6.5 feet tall. The average Israelite male in that time was 5'3", which means that Goliath would tower over his opponent either way.

The authors of Scripture don't usually comment on people's height, but in Samuel we have a few other pieces of data to consider. (1) The narrator tells us explicitly that Saul was head and shoulders above his peers, which suggests that he was over six feet tall (1 Samuel 9:2; 10:23). (2) When Samuel anointed David, God specifically said, "Do not consider his appearance or his height" (1 Samuel 16:7). As he was the youngest of his brothers, it's likely that the others were taller than he was.

When I teach this passage in class, I enjoy recruiting student volunteers to provide a visual aid. Usually, I have at least one student who is over six feet tall and another who is 5'3". Standing side by side at the front of the classroom, one student is a full head taller than the other. It's a powerful image. When Goliath issued his challenge, King Saul had the clear advantage over every other Israelite. His height was likely comparable to Goliath's.

Unlike the men in his army, Saul even had armor. The Philistines had monopolized the blacksmith industry, so Saul and Jonathan alone could afford armor (1 Samuel 13:22). We find this out when he tries to dress David with it (1 Samuel 17:38-39). Perhaps Saul felt guilty about not going himself. Or maybe he was hoping that people would mistake David for him.

The armor doesn't fit David, so he leaves it behind. David heads to the valley with no weapons aside from his sling. He is angered by Goliath's defiance of "the armies of the living God" and confident because God has already proved his faithfulness time and again as he watched over his sheep: "The LORD who rescued me from the paw of the lion and the paw of the bear will rescue me from the hand of this Philistine" (1 Samuel 17:36-37).

Facing Goliath with just five smooth stones and his sling, David is undeterred. He understands that the battle is not his. It is God's. His voice echoes through the valley: "You come against me with sword and spear and javelin, but I come against you in the name of the LORD Almighty, the God of the armies of Israel, whom you have defied" (1 Samuel 17:45).

David's victory over Goliath leads to national victory for Israel. Saul's son Jonathan, who is first in line for the kingship after his father, gives David his robe, tunic, sword, bow, and belt, symbolizing his acknowledgment that David should inherit the throne instead (1 Samuel 18:4). Women come out from the villages to honor Saul's victory, but they feature David in the refrain: "Saul has slain his thousands, and David his tens of thousands" (1 Samuel 18:7). This song reverberates through the rest of Samuel. The residents of Gath (a foreign city) recite it in 1 Samuel 21:11 and the Philistines do so in 1 Samuel 29:5, which indicates that the song had been sung so often by both men and women of Israel that even foreigners had heard it.[7] It hit the top of the charts, so to speak.

David's victory over Goliath was not only a personal achievement but a national triumph. It vindicated Yahweh's might and rallied the kingdom in celebration. The point was not David's age or size or strength but his absolute trust in Yahweh and his concern for Yahweh's reputation. David is a team player. He is among those in the Israelite community who trust God to intervene on behalf of his people and who are therefore empowered to act in alignment with God's purposes.

RIZPAH'S PROTEST

Sometimes the faith community is oblivious to injustice, so we must act alone to make things right. What can one person do in the face of a great wrong? David is deeply disturbed by Goliath's audacity in defying Yahweh. His passionate response wins the victory for the whole nation. He comes from the fields to the battle, though he is not a soldier himself. However, David is not always as sensitive as he should be to the plight of others. A little-known woman later during David's reign makes a singular difference. By her passionate response to injustice, she draws public attention to an unresolved problem. The story is multilayered, so to understand how her action exposes David's blind spot, we'll need to set the backdrop.

Second Samuel 21 begins with a predicament. David's people have endured three years of famine. God had warned that one consequence for Israel's disobedience would be crop failure (Leviticus 26:18-20). When David asks Yahweh what they have done to displease him, Yahweh responds, "It is on account of Saul and his blood-stained house; it is because he put the Gibeonites to death" (2 Samuel 21:1).

To understand why this is a problem, we must turn all the way back to the book of Joshua, when Israel first entered the land of Canaan. Yahweh warns Israel not to make alliances with people of the land because it will interfere with divine orders to drive out the inhabitants. Locals living in the town of Gibeon (thus called Gibeonites, though they were ethnically Hivites) do not want to leave their land (Joshua 11:9). They understand that Israel is under orders from Yahweh to drive them out, so they engage in trickery. They load their donkeys with worn-out sacks and cracked wineskins, put on their oldest, worn-out clothes and sandals, gather old bread, and hike to the Israelite camp not far away, pretending to have come a very long distance.

Without first seeking God's will, the Israelites decide that since Yahweh has not prohibited them from making alliances with nations far away, they can agree to a treaty with the Gibeonites, promising not to harm each other. Within a few days they learn that they have been tricked, but a promise made cannot be broken. According to the book of Joshua, after that the Gibeonites lived among the Israelites as woodcutters and water carriers.

Fast-forward to the reign of King Saul. The Bible does not recount for us the story of Saul's covenant violation, but at some point, he takes up the sword against Israel's sworn allies. By the time God confronts David with this, Saul has been dead for at least ten years. The story takes place vaguely "during the reign of David" without further specification, but it involves Gibeon, which is not in the initial territory over which David ruled from Hebron. David is king over Judah for 7.5 years before all Israel crowns him (2 Samuel 2:11). Add three years of famine, and it's been quite some time since Saul was king.

At least ten years later, Israel is still reaping the consequences of its previous ruler's foolishness. Yahweh explicitly indicates that he has sent a famine because of a covenant violation that took place long before David was king.

David acts immediately, summoning the surviving Gibeonites to find out how to make things right. They ask for the execution of seven of Saul's male descendants. Saul is already dead, so the only way to implement the death penalty is to cut off his descendants—a way of ensuring that Saul's line will not endure. The plan is not a divine command but rather the request of Saul's victims for revenge.

David accepts their plan without consulting Yahweh. He identifies seven descendants—five sons of Saul's daughter Merab and two sons of Saul's concubine, Rizpah. The Gibeonites kill these men and expose their bodies in a field, the ultimate form of dishonor. Both mothers have been pawns in the political drama of Saul's kingdom. Saul had tried to give Merab to David in marriage as a reward for his military success, but David refused her, so she was given to another man (1 Samuel 18:17-19). Rizpah was a secondary wife of Saul, with no inheritance rights. After she had borne sons for Saul, his commander, Abner, had allegedly raped her after Saul's death—a typical way that men in ancient times exerted their claim to the throne (2 Samuel 3:8).

Now, with her husband long dead, her sons murdered, and her dignity violated, Rizpah has nothing left to preserve but the honor of her family. For six months, she keeps vigil day and night over the bodies of her sons and step-grandsons in the field, making sure that birds of prey and wild animals do not come near them. She sleeps on sackcloth, and word of her public protest makes it back to King David, who responds by burying their bones in Saul's family tomb.

Notably, the narrator tells us, "*After that*, God answered prayer in behalf of the land" (2 Samuel 21:14). In other words, it wasn't enough to reconcile with the Gibeonites and avenge their wrong. Two wrongs do not make a right. The ongoing public shaming of Saul's sons and grandsons is excessive, as is the awful burden it places on their mothers. The exposed corpses are a source of ongoing trauma.

Rizpah's willingness to hold the public gaze day in and day out, calling attention to injustice, catalyzes a lasting solution to a problem that plagued the whole nation. While her pain is especially acute, the famine affects everyone. They bear shared responsibility to set things right again. God takes our commitments seriously. If we don't, we're in trouble.

Just ask Rizpah. Sociologist Christine Jeske considers current news stories that bring attention to violence or unfair treatment of others. She wonders, "When the news cycle shifts to the next tragedy, will we maintain the resolve it takes to deconstruct lies and dismantle systems [that disadvantage others]? Do we have Rizpah's resolve to lay our sackcloth on a rock and hold the public's focus until justice is done?"[8]

> God takes our commitments seriously. If we don't, we're in trouble.

MAKING AMENDS

Some Christians are nervous about the topic of intergenerational consequences for sin. Everyone agrees that people occasionally treat one another unjustly, but it's another thing to claim that the descendants of those who act unjustly are responsible to make it right. Am I responsible for what my ancestors have done? If so, how far back does that go, and how closely must I be related to them? A friend of ours recently discovered that his ancestors owned slaves. What is his responsibility toward the descendants of slaves today? My own grandparents clearly held racist attitudes. In her dementia, my grandmother kept repeating her favorite line: "If you're not Dutch, you're not much." What does that mean for me? As I was mulling over this question of intergenerational responsibility for sin, I stumbled on the story of Rizpah. It stopped me in my tracks.

King Saul abuses his power to take advantage of a vulnerable population that his ancestors pledged to protect. Saul doesn't make the covenant himself, but he inherits it when he becomes king. That means he is responsible to take it seriously. When he doesn't, grave consequences plague the entire nation. David hasn't done anything to harm the Gibeonites, and yet he inherits the consequences of Saul's foolhardy actions. David is responsible to do something about a problem he did not create.

We lived in Canada for four years. Just as we were moving back to the States in the summer of 2021, ground-penetrating radar discovered what appear to be unmarked burials of 215 children at the former site of the Kamloops Indian Residential School in British Columbia, a site to which First Nations children were forcibly taken. The Catholic Church operated the school from 1890 until 1969. This school and others like it across Canada, usually operated by churches, were known for "neglect and maltreatment" of children, some of whom suffered horrific abuse.[a] Over 150,000 children were taken to these schools for forced assimilation, and "thousands of children never made it home."[b] To save money, government policy dictated that children be buried on site without headstones rather than returning them to their families. Perhaps the graves were originally marked by wooden crosses but fell into disrepair when the schools closed.[c]

Some say the claims about mistreatment at these residential schools are overblown.[d] Others point out that no bones have been unearthed. Until they are, we must rely mainly on the testimonies of survivors. Some 60 percent of residential schools in Canada were run by the Catholic Church. In the summer of 2022, a year after the discovery of the burials, the pope made a visit to Canada to listen to the stories of survivors and to apologize for "the deplorable conduct of church members involved in residential schools."[e]

Pope Francis began his papacy in 2013, decades after the closure of the last of the residential schools. Some criticized Pope Francis for apologizing for something he did not do. However, he understood his responsibility as representative of the Catholic Church to make amends. In addition to the story of David and Rizpah, the Bible includes other examples of collective confessions (such as Nehemiah 9).

An apology is not enough on its own. Other steps toward restoration must follow. What those should be can be complicated to decide. However, if we take Scripture seriously, we must recognize that the sins of our ancestors can have ongoing consequences. We may be able to help resolve the injustices of the past. Our first task is to listen well to the stories of those who have been wronged. As God's family, we are called to care about harm others have experienced. We must learn how our own ancestors may have contributed to injustice against others. This responsibility is not limited to our biological family history but to our shared history as believers in Jesus and as members of institutions (churches, schools,

etc.). As Christians who believe in repentance and righteousness, we should lead the way in imagining how to generously
offer restorative justice to those inside our communities as
well as those who have been wronged by our communities,
even if we were not personally responsible for that harm.

SOLOMON'S GLORY

David's son Solomon is the last of the three kings who rules over all
Israel. His crowning achievement is building a permanent temple
in Jerusalem. Because we're tracking the presence of God in the Old
Testament as it shows up in the community of faith, it's important
to consider his story.

Let's be real. Solomon is—by any account—a complicated figure.
According to Deuteronomy 17:14-20, the king is not to "acquire great
numbers of horses for himself" or "take many wives" or "accumulate
large amounts of silver and gold." Can we agree that a yearly acquisi-
tion of twenty-five tons of gold is a bit over the top (1 Kings 10:14),
that twelve thousand horses constitute a "great number" of them
(1 Kings 10:26), and that taking seven hundred wives and three hundred concubines qualifies as excessive (1 Kings 11:3)? Although these
features would have brought Solomon great honor on the international scene, they prove his disobedience to Yahweh. As Moses and
Samuel both feared the kings would do, Solomon conscripts forced
labor for his building projects, and his foreign wives lead him astray
(1 Kings 9:15; 11:3; see Deuteronomy 17:14-20; 1 Samuel 8:10-18).

Still, Solomon builds a fabulous temple. Despite his efforts, he
cannot control God's response. He must pray and wait for God to
act. On the day the priests bring the covenant chest into the most
holy place, the glory of Yahweh fills the temple, indicating Yahweh's
authorization of this place of worship (1 Kings 8:10-11). As an echo
of the presence of God in the tabernacle at Sinai (Exodus 40), this

moment is laden with significance. The same God who had descended the mountain to live among his people puts his stamp of approval on Solomon's temple. Israel again has God's presence in their midst. God's presence is the greatest gift of all.

The temple dedication is elaborate. Solomon genuinely desires the favor of Yahweh on the land of Israel. His prayer appeals to God's mercy, asking him to hear the prayers of those who will gather there, even when those gathered are foreigners who come from distant lands to pray to Yahweh (1 Kings 8:41-43). Solomon recognizes that the worship of Yahweh will have international appeal and that non-Jews will desire to approach Yahweh in prayer.

> God's presence is the greatest gift of all.

King Solomon's elaborate dedication lasts fourteen days, and all Israel participates, "a vast assembly" (an *ekklēsia*, 1 Kings 8:65). He sacrifices an enormous number of fellowship offerings, the meat of which would have been shared with those who gathered—a massive feast indeed. The temple is good news for the entire nation, so everyone is present to acknowledge the significance of this moment.

Yahweh appears to Solomon in response to his prayer, saying, "My eyes and my heart will always be there" (1 Kings 9:3). God also issues a warning for Solomon and the nation to obey his commands. If they fail to do this, then Yahweh will reject the temple and send them into exile. It's an ominous warning. Yahweh has already witnessed the dysfunction of the royal family (remember, Solomon's mother is Bathsheba, the wife of Uriah!) and national apostasy. If they want to enjoy the ongoing blessing of God's presence, they need to recommit themselves corporately to covenant faithfulness.

Individual obedience is important, but no one person can carry the nation alone. This is a group project. We are at our best when we are gathered to faithfully worship God together.

KEY IDEAS

- The inclusion of Samuel in the priesthood shows us that God can select anyone for his service, regardless of family background.
- The abundance we enjoy is God's invitation to partner with him to ensure that everyone has what they need.
- Our communities bear shared responsibility to set things right when we or our ancestors have broken our commitments.
- The greatest gift we can receive when we are gathered to faithfully worship God together is God's own presence.

DIGGING DEEPER

Stephanie Buckhanon Crowder. *When Momma Speaks: The Bible and Motherhood from a Womanist Perspective*. Westminster John Knox, 2016.

David G. Firth. "They Sang and They Celebrated: The Women's Celebration in 1 Samuel 18:7." *Bulletin for Biblical Research* 33, no. 4 (2023): 476-88.

Denise C. Flanders. "The Reversal of (Food) Injustice: The Song of Hannah (1 Sam 2:1-20)." *Bulletin for Biblical Research* 33, no. 4 (2023): 458-75.

Related videos from BibleProject: "Justice," "Generosity," and "1 & 2 Kings."

4

DIVIDED FAMILY

ANONYMOUS PROPHETS

The glory of Solomon's temple dedication is in a way short-lived. During his lifetime, one of Solomon's officials, by the name of Jeroboam, rebels against him and takes refuge in Egypt. Because Solomon has begun worshiping foreign gods, Yahweh determines to take most of the kingdom away from Solomon's son, leaving him only the tribe of Judah (1 Kings 11). As soon as Solomon dies, the kingdom splits in two over the folly of his son Rehoboam.

Jeroboam sees his opportunity and heads north from Egypt, making Shechem his capital and thereby establishing the Northern Kingdom of Israel. Before long, he cleverly consolidates his power by installing two golden calves, one at the northern edge of his kingdom (in Dan) and the other at the southern edge (in Bethel). This makes it unnecessary for the Israelites to travel south to the temple in Jerusalem to worship and spend their shekels. Jeroboam doesn't even try to hide the fact that he's taking inspiration from the golden calf episode at Mount Sinai in Exodus 32. He quotes Aaron's apostasy openly, saying, "Here are your gods, Israel, who brought you up out

of Egypt" (1 Kings 12:28). As if that weren't enough, he names his son
Nadab after Aaron's rebellious son (1 Kings 14:20; see Leviticus 10:1-3).[1]
Nostalgia can be very problematic if it revives unsavory behavior.

Figure 4.1. Map of Dan and Bethel

Unfortunately, Jeroboam's innovation was replicated by many of
Israel's kings, who perpetuated the "sins of Jeroboam" (e.g.,
1 Kings 16:31; 2 Kings 3:3). Those who carried on his legacy were
responsible for the vulnerability of the kingdom of Israel to the
Assyrian army (2 Kings 17:22-23).

Campaign slogans usually lean forward, promising a sparkling vision of what the nation can become under new leadership, but sometimes politicians call for a return to the past. Warren G. Harding's 1920 bid for the presidency called for a "Return to Normalcy" after World War I. In a similar vein, Franklin D. Roosevelt announced in 1932, "Happy Days Are Here Again." In retrospect, Roosevelt's optimism was obviously misplaced—the Great Depression lasted nine more years, giving way to World War II. These leaders felt that something positive about America's past had been lost and needed to be recovered. In any age, nostalgic slogans must lead to clear articulation about which aspects of the past are worth retrieving or reviving. What era was characterized by happy days? Colonial times? Slavery? The Civil War? The Great Depression? World Wars? Jim Crow? Not everyone has rosy memories of America's past. What was great for some was not great for everyone.

Years ago, I met regularly with a Jehovah's Witness in hopes of sharing the truth of Scripture with her (she had the same hopes for me). When she explained her view that Jesus was not divine but only human, I responded that the historic witness of the church was clear on this. The apostles, councils, and creeds all affirmed Jesus' deity alongside his humanity. Her response took me by surprise: "But there has always been a remnant of those who held to the truth." She cited Arius as one shining example—a man whom the church condemned as a heretic for his views at the Council of Nicaea in 325 CE. My friend's historical precedent was my heretic!

Jeroboam's goal is to build a new dynasty that can claim continuity with the past, but he's looking in all the wrong places for inspiration. He reaches back into the archives for an alternative to the covenant with Yahweh, finding solidarity with Aaron's behavior at Mount Sinai.[2] His apostasy is clear. He appoints priests who are not from the tribe of Levi and sets his own festival calendar, ignoring the Torah regulations. All this sets the scene for a strange encounter between two anonymous prophets. It's a cautionary tale with significant theological implications. It will make the most sense if you take time to read 1 Kings 13 first.

I'm sure the characters in this chapter had names, but the narrator calls them only "a man of God" from Judah and "a certain old prophet" living in Bethel. Even Jeroboam is usually just called "the king" in this chapter. That anonymity proves important: their behavior becomes a paradigm for future generations.

Here's the short version of the story: A prophet from Judah goes north to Bethel to prophesy against Jeroboam's new altar, where the golden calf is set up. Jeroboam orders his guards to seize the prophet, but his outstretched hand instantly shrivels and the altar splits in two, which puts a stop to the arrest. At the king's request, the prophet prays for his hand to be healed (and it is), but the prophet refuses to go home and eat with Jeroboam because Yahweh has warned him not to eat with anyone in Israel.

As the man of God heads home, an "old prophet" living in Bethel meets him on the way and invites him home for a meal. The old prophet tricks the man of God into thinking it is God's will that they eat together, so the man of God from Judah lets his guard down. Afterward, on his way home, the man of God is mauled by a lion. The old prophet gathers his bones and buries the man in his own tomb, asking his sons to one day bury him by the man's side.

It's a bizarre story, really. I'm thankful for Peter Leithart's insightful commentary that finally helped me figure out what is going on. By not naming the characters, the narrator draws our attention to locations, so that each of the prophets comes to represent their country—the man of God represents Judah, and the old prophet represents Israel.[3] In Leithart's words, "Judah remains for centuries as a prophetic witness against the northern kingdom, but at some time, Israel seduces Judah as the old prophet seduces the man of God from Judah. Eventually, the two nations will be united in death, in the grave of exile."[4] Not every biblical story works parabolically like this, but narrative clues suggest that this is the way we should understand 1 Kings 13.

The man of God had prophesied that Jeroboam's altar would split in two and that someday a king named Josiah would burn the bones of the renegade priests on their own altar (1 Kings 13:3). The altar splits that very day, but the other part of his prophetic word is not fulfilled until 2 Kings 23. At that time, Josiah institutes reforms, including the desecration and dismantling of all the altars Israel and Judah's kings set up to false gods. At Bethel, Josiah takes the bones of the unfaithful priests out of their tombs and burns them on the altar to desecrate the bones and defile the altar. But he does not disturb the bones of the man of God and the old prophet out of respect for their faith in Yahweh (2 Kings 23:15-18).

This chapter is a cautionary tale for God's people with relevance for us today. The only way to survive the threat of God's judgment was to listen to the faithful witness of the prophets of Judah and to stay true to the word of Yahweh, refusing to be seduced by unfaithful forms of worship in Israel. The old prophet, corrupt though he was, trusted the word of the man of God from Judah enough to put his dead bones beside him. That act of faith prevented his own bones from desecration.

We're focusing in this book on God's intentions for believers to form a faithful community where God's presence is welcome. Our vision for the community matters. A community built around false worship or nostalgia for an unfaithful past will self-destruct.

A community built around false worship or nostalgia for an unfaithful past will self-destruct.

MAKING SENSE OF THE DIVIDED KINGDOM

It can be hard to keep track of who's who and what's what when reading the Old Testament, especially after the nation of Israel divides in two. If Israel's history is fuzzy to us, we can easily get lost.

As a child, I had a hard time keeping track of our extended family members. My dad is an only child, but he has seventy-two first cousins because both of his parents belonged to large families with many children and grandchildren. Part of what made it especially challenging for me to keep track of aunts and uncles and cousins is that my grandmother would refer to them in multiple ways. Not only were there a multitude of people to know, but each one had alternate names! If she heard from her niece Jane, she might report, "Nice Avenue called." Or "I got a letter from Mentone." Or "All is well in Ontario." Never mind that she had relatives in Ontario, California, *and* Ontario, Canada. We were just supposed to know which one she meant.

Reading the Bible can be exactly like this. In a few places, *Israel* refers to the patriarch Jacob, using his new name. More commonly, *Israel* means the entire nation that came out of Egypt, while at other times, *Israel* refers only to the Northern Kingdom after it broke away from Judah following the death of Solomon. Then again, to make it even more confusing, after the exile of the Northern Kingdom sometimes *Israel* denotes Judah!

I found this so complicated that I finally made myself a cheat sheet to help me track with what I'm reading. I share it here with you in hopes that it will help you too. But first, a few pointers:

- The books of 1–2 Samuel take place during the united monarchy, when Saul and then David are king over all

Israel (mostly, except for a few years when Saul's son Ishbosheth rules over the northern tribes).

- In 1 Kings 1–11, Solomon becomes king over all Israel and builds the temple in Jerusalem.

- After Solomon's death, the kingdom splits in two, with Jeroboam ruling the northern tribes (known as Israel), and Rehoboam ruling the southern tribes (Judah, Benjamin, and Simeon, which all become known as Judah). All the kings of Judah are descendants of David, and they reign from Jerusalem, which is sometimes called Zion (especially in poetic contexts).

- From 1 Kings 12 to 2 Kings 17, the storyline focuses on the Northern Kingdom. We hear bits and pieces about Judah, but Israel is the focus until they are carried off into exile by the Assyrians. The capital of the Northern Kingdom is the city of Samaria, and its largest landholdings belong to the tribes of Ephraim and Manasseh, the sons of Joseph.

- The rest of 2 Kings (2 Kings 18–25) focuses on the Southern Kingdom of Judah until they are taken into exile by the Babylonian army. Its capital remains in Jerusalem.

- The books of Chronicles cover the same period as 2 Samuel through 2 Kings. Fifty percent of Chronicles is taken directly from Samuel and Kings. However, the Chronicler focuses especially on the Southern Kingdom of Judah, rather than the Northern Kingdom of Israel, because his aim is to follow the Davidic line of kings. The new material relates especially to the kings of Judah, the temple priests, and anything that connects these two, such as temple renovations or festivals or prayers.

With all that in mind, here's a list of titles to watch for, often used interchangeably, along with whom they represent:

Southern Kingdom	Northern Kingdom
Judah	Israel
David	Joseph
Jerusalem	Samaria
Zion	Ephraim

UNLIKELY COUNCIL

Community can be a good thing, but we enter a danger zone when we surround ourselves with people who will only tell us what we want to hear. If our friends or advisers are unwilling to sound the alarm when they see us making poor choices, then we do not have the right advisers.

The track record of the Northern Kingdom of Israel is uniformly bad. One king after another supports the worship of foreign gods and gives himself over to drunkenness and violence. King Ahab takes rebellion to the next level, sponsoring the worship of Baal and Asherah by building them a temple and bankrolling their prophets. After twenty-two years as king, Ahab meets with Jehoshaphat, king of Judah, and enlists his help in attacking the neighboring nation of Aram. Ahab has clashed swords with Aram on more than one occasion. His goal is to take back land that used to belong to Israel.

Jehoshaphat, whose name means "Yahweh judges," is amenable to the idea of going into battle but suggests that they should inquire first to see whether they have Yahweh's favor. His suggestion turns out to be halfhearted, because he goes to battle even after an unfavorable outcome is announced. But I'm getting ahead of myself. Let's set the scene for the inquiry:

Ahab gathers not one, not two, but four hundred prophets, asking, "Shall I go to war . . . or shall I refrain?" Their answer is unanimous: "Go . . . for the Lord will give it into the king's hand" (1 Kings 22:6).

Now, let's stop for a moment to consider their words carefully. Notice that the prophets do not use God's personal name, Yahweh (which would have been rendered LORD in small capital letters in English), instead using the generic title "Lord" (*Adonai* in Hebrew). Notice, too, that they do not name the king. Into *which* king's hand will the land be given? Their "prophetic" announcement is vague enough that they are right either way.

Have you ever read a horoscope? Or the slip of paper in a fortune cookie? They are notoriously vague and subject to any number of interpretations. Inspirational talks and even sermons can be like this too. Pump enough ambiguity into a message, and the hearer can hear whatever they want to hear. That's what happens in Ahab's throne room.

Jehoshaphat sees right through this. Despite the crowd, he asks, "Is there no longer a prophet of Yahweh here whom we can inquire of?" (1 Kings 22:7).

Ahab's answer is oh-so-telling: "There is still one prophet through whom we can inquire of Yahweh, but I hate him because he never prophesies anything good about me, but always bad. He is Micaiah son of Imlah." Ahab is more interested in unconditional support than he is in godly counsel.

This cautionary tale is meant to warn us against the dangers of living in an echo chamber of our own making. As Peter Leithart admits, "It is always a temptation to prefer a smooth, self-affirming word over a confronting word, and that temptation has been institutionalized, systematized in many contemporary churches."[5]

While they wait for the arrival of Micaiah, the other prophets suddenly begin prophesying in Yahweh's name and offering much more specific messages. They've picked up on the fact that the visiting dignitary is not yet convinced. The messenger sent to get Micaiah advises him what to say so that his words align with the others (the audacity!). And then, surprisingly, Micaiah announces the same thing as the false prophets. Ahab was not expecting that outcome, so he prods further, and Micaiah finally unloads his vision from Yahweh: certain defeat awaits them in battle.

Then the prophet offers a glimpse into the heavenly throne room, where Yahweh reveals his plan to entice Ahab to attack Aram so that he will die in battle. As it turns out, the lying prophets are under God's sovereignty. God uses their willingness to tell the king whatever he wants to hear to lure him to his death.

Considering Micaiah's sober words, it is remarkable that Ahab and Jehoshaphat proceed with their plans to go into battle. Taking a page from the Assyrian playbook, Ahab devises a plan. In Assyria, if a prophet announces a bad omen for the king, the king will remove his robes, dress a servant in them, and perform a ritual to make the servant a substitute king so that the terrible fate will befall the servant instead of the true king. Ahab removes his robes and enters battle, hoping that the defending army will instead kill Jehoshaphat, who is gullible enough to agree to Ahab's plan by going into battle in his kingly garb.

But Yahweh's plan cannot be thwarted so easily. A soldier shoots king Ahab at random with an arrow, not knowing he is king. By the end of the battle, Ahab is dead and his army scattered (1 Kings 22:37-38).

It takes tremendous effort to pursue the truth about ourselves rather than to surround ourselves with people who will stroke our ego and rubber-stamp our ideas. When we become part of God's family, our shared task is to pursue God's will together. To do that we must become a community that speaks truth to each other in love (Ephesians 4:25). God's goal for humanity from the beginning is that we would be allies in carrying out the work to which God has called us.

> When we become part of God's family, our shared task is to pursue God's will together.

DESPERATE TIMES

Aside from his foolish military exploit with the wicked Israelite king Ahab, King Jehoshaphat of Judah was a good king. He prayed to Yahweh rather than false gods and made efforts to teach the covenant throughout the land (2 Chronicles 17). He appointed and instructed judges, calling on them to serve Yahweh faithfully—an appropriate endeavor for a man whose name means "Yahweh judges" (2 Chronicles 19).

Late in his reign, Jehoshaphat faces a challenge that causes him deep alarm. Three enemy nations ally themselves and are marching to meet him in battle. By the time he hears about it, they are already near (2 Chronicles 20). His knee-jerk reaction shows us just how much he has been formed by faithful worship: "Jehoshaphat resolved to inquire of the LORD, and he proclaimed a fast for all Judah" (2 Chronicles 20:3). He does not seek God by himself. The whole nation joins him in it, gathering at the temple they have just renovated. There, Jehoshaphat prays publicly, recalling God's powerful work on behalf of previous generations and reminding God of Solomon's temple dedication prayer: "If calamity comes upon us, whether the sword of judgment, or plague or famine, we will stand in your presence before this temple that bears your Name and will cry out to you in our distress, and you will hear us and save us" (2 Chronicles 20:9). Then Jehoshaphat honestly describes the coming attackers. He admits, "We have no power to face this vast army that is attacking us. We do not know what to do, but our eyes are on you" (2 Chronicles 20:12). The narrator reminds us that the entire community, young and old, male and female, stands there to witness this desperate plea. They share his sense of alarm. They have no answers.

I wonder how often this happens in our churches today—honest prayers of desperation expressed publicly in expectation that God will hear and act. Many of our churches would consider this level of vulnerability too messy for a Sunday service. The attention of our leaders is often directed at those who walk in the door, wanting to give them a good, inspirational experience rather than joining them in seeking God. Do we avoid lament? Do we corporately fail to admit when we're in over our head because we want to exude confidence? Do we use our services to manage our brand rather than approaching God with authenticity? This approach inadvertently sends the message to Christians that faith requires certainty and confidence. Perhaps we have forgotten why we gather. What would happen if we prayed the truth?

What could God do in our midst if we came with heartfelt pleas to heal the political divides that fracture our families and churches? What healing would be unleashed if we interceded for struggling marriages or for those battling depression and anxiety by presenting these crises to God? What could the Spirit do with a community that is honest about our propensities toward distraction or the numbness we feel toward the world's problems? What if we prayed together in desperation for an end to the wars that ravage the nations of our world?

> What would happen if we prayed the truth?

This story ends in jubilation. A prophet speaks up in response to Jehoshaphat's brutal honesty before God, reassuring the people that Yahweh will fight the battle for them. He echoes the words of Moses to the people of Israel when they stood at the sea with the army of Pharaoh bearing down on them: "Do not be afraid or discouraged because of this vast army. For the battle is not yours, but God's. . . . You will not have to fight this battle. Take up your positions; stand firm and see the deliverance the LORD will give you" (2 Chronicles 20:15, 17; see Exodus 14:13). And then they do the next logical thing: they worship.

Considering what they have learned, it doesn't make sense to suit up in armor or sharpen their swords. They fall down in worship, expressing thanks to the God who heard their prayer and will do for them what they cannot do for themselves.

Jehoshaphat is so convinced of the prophet's message that the next morning, as they set out to meet the approaching army, he puts a choir at the head of the army. Imagine! By the time they arrive on the scene, the three enemy armies have already decimated each other. The men of Judah return home singing, their arms loaded with plunder from the invaders. God's supernatural victory is unmistakable.

The Bible does not present us with a pull-yourself-up-by-your-bootstraps religion or a look-on-the-bright-side approach to life. By bearing witness to the struggles of ordinary people, it helps us to recognize our own limitations. This story of a nation in crisis models for us a communal posture of dependence on God and invites us to cultivate a zone of authenticity rather than bravado in our gatherings. Think of what Jehoshaphat would have missed if he simply rushed into battle in his own strength. Think of what we miss when we do.

VISION RESTORED

The Southern Kingdom of Judah had more than its fair share of kings who cared little about the worship of Yahweh. Of the twenty or so kings of Judah, only eight of them sought to be faithful to the covenant. One of these eight led the nation during a season of repentance and restoration.

Josiah was only eight years old when his father Amon was assassinated, and he suddenly became king (2 Chronicles 34). Amon was trouble, and he lasted only two years as king. Idol worship was Amon's obsession. If we do the math, we discover that Amon must have fathered Josiah when he was only sixteen years old. Men of Israel did not marry that young, so Josiah is likely the product of youthful passion. Perhaps Josiah is too young to absorb his father's waywardness. Perhaps his mother trains him well. Whatever the reason, Josiah breaks with his father's tradition and makes King David his model. It's another example of God redeeming a messy family.

At twenty-six, Josiah authorizes temple renovations, hiring those skilled with wood and stone to fix what has gone into disrepair. In the process, the high priest finds a scroll—the words of which send shock waves through the community. It turns out that the scroll is some portion of the Torah. We don't know how much of the Torah they find (many suspect it is the core of Deuteronomy), but it is enough to let them know that they are in hot water. Because their ancestors have forsaken Yahweh and worshiped other gods, they have angered God and will face his judgment.

One detail in this story that is often overlooked is that when they find the scroll and need someone to inquire of God about it, they go to a prophet named Huldah. These are the days of the prophet Jeremiah, so Huldah is not their only option. She is a married woman apparently known for reliably speaking on Yahweh's behalf. Despite other options, they choose a woman to interpret God's Word. Huldah speaks boldly regarding their sin, God's anger, and his mercy in response to their repentance. This story offers a glimpse of God's intention for faithful communities in which men and women collaborate in listening to and obeying God.

Josiah's response is immediate. He gathers the leaders along with all the people of Judah. He reads them the scroll and leads them in renewing the covenant in God's presence. Josiah understands that it isn't enough to privately commit to honoring God. The Lord's instructions are intended to shape the entire community. The public reading of Scripture galvanizes Judah. As the people give shared attention to God's Word, they rediscover their purpose.

Shared attention is a powerful medium to catalyze change. We live in a world where our focus is fractured in a thousand ways. It's increasingly rare for families to sit and watch the same show or read the same book. Instead, we huddle over our own screens that serve up individualized entertainment in the form of social media posts, news sites, games, chatrooms, or streaming services. Even a couple on a date may sit on opposite sides of the table staring at their phones instead of each other. One result is that we drift further away (mentally and emotionally) from those with whom we share physical space. When we aren't hearing the same news or laughing at the same jokes, we lose the connective tissue that binds us.

To gather with others and give our collective attention to one thing is becoming unusual. Sure, we do so at the movie theater or with a concert or dramatic production or sporting event, but the crowds for these events are not committed to one another. We may experience a brief sense of solidarity, but it fades as soon as we head home. When our congregation gathers for worship week after week, we are participating in something truly radical. To sing and pray together, hear Scripture read and preached, to witness baptisms, to give of our resources, and to share in the ritual of Communion, remembering what Christ has done to reconcile us to God and to each other—these are the powerful means by which we are collectively transformed. This is how we become God's family.

Josiah's instinct is to gather everyone to hear the Word. For a matter this important, they need to look one another in the eye and commit together to making drastic changes. The passion or vision of one person is not enough. After hearing the contents of the scroll, the people sign on, pledging themselves to the covenant. And then they act. Over time, the people of Judah have tolerated more and more practices associated with false gods. Jerusalem is filled with monuments, and the hills around the city have numerous "high places" devoted to false gods. This is why the words of the scroll are so alarming.

"You shall have no other gods before me. You shall not make for yourself an image in the form of anything in heaven above or on the earth beneath or in the waters below" (Deuteronomy 5:7-8). Josiah gets right to work destroying idols and removing priests who are dedicated to facilitating the worship of the gods represented by those idols. He dismantles religious prostitution and other industries centered on idolatry. He tears down and desecrates religious sites and burns the bones of priests who devoted themselves to false worship.

That's when he comes across the bones of the anonymous prophet from 1 Kings 13, whose story I told earlier. The Northern Kingdom has already gone into exile, giving Josiah access to some of the land that had been theirs. Josiah's altar-smashing campaign takes him to Bethel, across the northern border of Judah. Josiah asks, "What is that tombstone I see?"

They answer, "It marks the tomb of the man of God who came from Judah and pronounced against the altar of Bethel the very things you have done to it."

"'Leave it alone,' he said. 'Don't let anyone disturb his bones.' So, they spared his bones and those of the prophet who had come from Samaria" (2 Kings 23:17-18).

After all this necessary work, they celebrate the Passover together for the first time in years. Josiah's reign is a bright spot in a long string of disasters. He understands that to experience God's blessing, Judah needs to become a community committed to proper worship with shared attention to the Word of God and a shared commitment to faithful obedience. Unfortunately, the wickedness of those who came before him and the wickedness of those who come after him determine their fate: exile.

KEY IDEAS

- A community build around false worship will self-destruct.
- Our shared task as the family of God is to pursue God's will together and to face the truth about ourselves. Our

communities should not become an echo chamber that will tell us what we want to hear.

- God invites us to come to him in a posture of dependence and expectation.

- When we give shared attention to God's Word and commit to obeying God's command, we rediscover our purpose.

DIGGING DEEPER

Wilda Gafney. *Womanist Midrash: A Reintroduction to the Women of the Torah and the Throne.* Westminster John Knox, 2017.
Peter Leithart. *1 & 2 Kings.* Brazos Theological Commentary on the Bible. Brazos, 2016.

Related videos from BibleProject: "The Prophets" and "Public Reading of Scripture."

5

KICKED OUT OF THE HOUSE

INDEPENDENCE DAY

I'm writing this on the Fourth of July, which is Independence Day in the United States. From every direction, I can hear explosions. Neighbors have set up lawn chairs, and children are giddy with excitement to see the colors and hear the pops and crackles and booms. My city holds its major fireworks event on July 3, presumably so that we can enjoy the shows put on by other cities in our area on July 4. The (illegal) private fireworks are every bit as large and impressive as the official ones, and they go on for much, much longer.

Perhaps because I've been immersed in writing this book, it strikes me as funny that our national holiday celebrates independence. To be American is to be free from "taxation without representation" under British rule, to be free to do whatever we want, as long as we don't hurt others. We prepare our children for adulthood by teaching them to do things by themselves, for themselves. In school, we test individual knowledge. We apply for jobs solo. Our performance evaluations are also solitary.

What if—instead of independence—we celebrated *inter*dependence? What if our holiday recognized how much we need each other? What if we spent more time training our children to work *together*, for the benefit of all, rather than to prove their self-sufficiency? What if we shared more of what we have and received what others have to offer?

> What if—instead of independence—we celebrated *inter*dependence?

It strikes me that independence was a problem from the early days in Eden. Adam and Eve sought autonomy from God. They wanted the freedom to decide for themselves what was right and wrong. The rest of us have been following suit ever since.

In chapter four, we explored the books of Kings and Chronicles, both of which narrate the stories of the monarchs of Israel and Judah, most of whom invested heavily in going their own way. Yahweh was patient for generation after generation, giving the nation every opportunity to turn things around. Eventually, like an exasperated parent, God gave them the autonomy they craved. *So, you don't want to live as my people and follow my rules? Fine. Get off my land!*

Their collective consequence was forced migration, though they didn't all leave. Many of them stayed behind, trying to eke out a living in a land stripped of its leadership and its central institutions, temple and throne. But while the displacement was physical for only some, it was painfully real for all. Nothing stayed as it had been. The losses of life and Israel's way of life were devastating.

Into the wreckage, God sent prophets. These men and women interpreted the losses of their contemporaries, trying to help them see how and why their lives had come unraveled. They also cast a vision for what God still planned to do—a vision of deep interdependence on God and one another. While their messages were not cheerful overall, their clear-eyed view of reality was the best form of love.

My friend Esau McCaulley, professor of New Testament at Wheaton College, wrote an opinion piece for the *New York Times* on America's Independence Day. As a Black man, Esau has seen the underside of our nation's inequalities and prejudice, and he is open about the ways that he and his family have suffered harm. He writes,

> Too often we worry that if we tell our children about our complex and sometimes dark history, their response will be debilitating shame. But instead of lying to our youth, we can give them a task that demands the best of them. We can call upon them to close the often-gaping chasm between our ideals and practices. This is the gift the past offers us, a chance to flee old evils and pursue new goods.[1]

This is precisely what the prophets of old did: they told the truth about their national predicament, and they called God's people to a better future.

They did it as they announced God's urgent messages for their generation, and they did it as they told and retold the stories of the past. In the Hebrew Bible, the narratives of Joshua, Judges, Samuel, and Kings are known as the "Former Prophets"—offering God's perspective on the years of their complicated history. We've already explored those books together. Then comes the "Latter Prophets"— collections of prophetic oracles given by Isaiah, Jeremiah, Ezekiel, and the Twelve.

In this chapter we'll consider the message of the prophets Jeremiah and Ezekiel as they spoke truth about Israel's sin and envisioned a better future for the whole nation. The road to restoration they prophesied was a surprise to just about everyone: a new way to worship, a path marked by suffering, and a deep investment in a land far from home. We'll also look at the lives of two people who found alternative ways to live faithfully in the heart of the empire: Daniel and Esther.

God's people may have been kicked out of their house, but it was not the end of their story. The possibility of restoration beckoned to those united by the message of the prophets. If they could come together around the truth of Yahweh's kingship, they could again become a nation where God's Spirit was present among them.

GARDENS IN BABYLON

The prophet Jeremiah had the unpleasant task of telling his contemporaries what they did not want to hear. He was an emotional man, freely admitting the deep grief he felt over his nation's waywardness. He resolutely refused to look on the bright side of things, pulling people's attention back time and again to their predicament and to the faults that got them there.

Jeremiah started his ministry on the verge of disaster. He lived through the earth-shattering trauma of the Babylonian invasion of Judah and destruction of Jerusalem. He watched as his nation's elite were led in chains to a land far, far away where they would live out their days wishing they could come home. The Babylonians didn't take everyone with them, only the court officials, leaders, skilled workers, and artisans. Jeremiah was left behind with the rabble the Babylonian government apparently found neither threatening nor useful. Those who remained managed to make Jeremiah's life miserable by ignoring his messages and forcing him to do things against his will. At one point, despite his protests, they dragged him to Egypt, where they thought the grass would be greener. (Clearly, they had forgotten their national history!)

Jeremiah and Ezekiel both had surprisingly little to say against Babylon. Ezekiel includes a whole section of prophetic oracles against the nations, but Babylon gets a free pass. For him, Babylon is a place of protection for the exiles. Jeremiah's book closes with two chapters of harsh warnings regarding Babylon's ultimate demise, but he begins his ministry with a different tune. Jeremiah's first message about Babylon is downright positive.

Jeremiah's insistence that Judah surrender to Nebuchadnezzar, king of Babylon, does not exactly make him popular: "Bow your neck under the yoke of the king of Babylon; serve him and his people, and you will live" (Jeremiah 27:12). For Jeremiah, as for Ezekiel and Isaiah, Babylon is a tool in the hand of Yahweh. Those who submit to Babylon will survive the whole ordeal. Those who resist will lose everything. How's that for a patriotic sermon?!

Eventually, the word of the Lord through Jeremiah comes true. Nebuchadnezzar sacks the city of Jerusalem and hauls off its treasures. Jeremiah follows up with the exiles in Babylon by writing them a letter. Can you imagine what such a letter might contain? We might expect him to urge repentance, awakening the hope that God would allow them to return. Or perhaps he would encourage them to escape, or to spy on the evil empire and undermine it in any way they can. At the very least, he will tell them to resist assimilation and reject Babylonian values, right?

Jeremiah does none of these things. Instead, he has vegetables, mud bricks, and weddings on his mind. Jeremiah's letter contains a specific word from Yahweh:

> Build houses and settle down; plant gardens and eat what they produce. Marry and have sons and daughters; find wives for your sons and give your daughters in marriage, so that they too may have sons and daughters. Increase in number there; do not decrease. Also, seek the peace and prosperity of the city to which I have carried you into exile. Pray to the LORD for it, because if it prospers, you too will prosper. (Jeremiah 29:5-7)

This letter is the closest we come to an authorized "prosperity gospel" in the whole Bible, and it undoubtedly shocked those who received it. To build a home in Babylon would be to admit to themselves and others that they were in it for the long haul. To plant gardens would be to unpack their bags and settle down like they belonged there. God tells them to tie themselves to the land and its people by getting married and bearing children—children for whom Babylon will feel like home. In other words, they are to keep on living. These activities were precisely the ones that constituted valid exemptions from going to war. If the nation went to war, but you had just built a house, planted a vineyard, or gotten married, then you were encouraged to stay home from the front lines to tend to your household (Deuteronomy 20:5-7).[2] The implication is that Yahweh does not want them to take an adversarial posture in Babylon but instead to cultivate a peace-time mindset.

Most unforeseen of all is Yahweh's instruction to "seek the peace and prosperity of the city to which I have carried you." That city is Babylon, the archenemy of God's people. The Jews are not supposed to dig trenches for battle or engage in subversive activities. They are to love their neighbors and live at peace with them. When the time comes to judge the Babylonian Empire, Yahweh will be the one to do it. The job of the exiles is to work and pray for the city and its inhabitants to flourish.

God nudged Jonathan Brooks to move back into the neglected urban neighborhood on the south side of Chicago where he grew up to start a church. Jonathan bought a house but admits now that at first, he avoided his neighbors because the neighborhood was not known to be "safe." In his book, *Church Forsaken: Practicing Presence in Neglected Neighborhoods*, Jonathan tells the story of his own gradual realization that presence and investment and friendship matter.[3] If we fear our own neighbors, we will never contribute to thriving neighborhoods.

I wonder what our world could look like if Christians took Jeremiah's approach. What if, instead of expending our energy to fight for our rights and protect our interests, we invested in the flourishing of our communities? What if the church

> If we fear our own neighbors, we will never contribute to thriving neighborhoods.

was right in the thick of things working for better schools and neighborhoods instead of withdrawing from them, organizing resources to benefit the health of our waterways and our parks, and talking to our neighbors instead of hiding from them? What if we planted gardens and started businesses?

In his book *Reading for the Common Good*, C. Christopher Smith tells the story of his own urban neighborhood in Indianapolis. Abandoned homes and businesses and a derelict school have been renovated and renewed. Chemical-soaked soil was rehabilitated so that new, sustainable low-income senior housing could be built. Community gardens, a gym, and a hockey rink are hubs of activity. New businesses have opened. Chris writes, "Working with our neighbors, our church has been deeply involved in all of these changes to our neighborhood. . . . Our aim has been to immerse ourselves in the story of God's reconciling work."[4]

A deep investment for the good of our communities creates healthy interdependence. Jesus calls us even to seek the prosperity of those we consider our enemies (Matthew 5:43-48). What if the church became a force for the common good?

SKATE RAMPS IN CHURCH?

Engaging in neighborhood outreach requires courage. We must be willing to unclench our fists because something could go wrong. The carpet could get stained. Someone could take advantage of our generosity. And what about our insurance liability?

One of the most inspiring ministry stories I know is the story of Central Bible Church in Portland, Oregon. CB, as it was known, was situated near Multnomah University. One of the students—Paul, a skateboarder from California—ran into some skaters who had snuck out of youth group in search of a good place to skate. Paul started meeting them to skate together in the church parking lot. Eventually, the staff of Central Bible agreed to let Paul and his buddy Clint turn the church basement into an indoor skate park. That involved building ramps and rails and letting a whole lot of unchurched kids through the church doors on a weekly basis to skateboard and hear the gospel. Paul happened to be an amazing Bible teacher. The Spirit used his messages to awaken thousands of young people to the love of God.

In 1996, while my husband and I were students at Multnomah, CB built a skate warehouse on the church property with the best half-pipes in town.[a] Our married student apartment looked out on that warehouse. Twice a week we could hear those skateboards rolling. Many of our college classmates were skaters training for ministry, thanks to the discipleship they had as teens at SkateChurch. I can think of at least five of them who went on to get PhDs in Old Testament. One of them is Tim Mackie, cofounder of BibleProject, one of my favorite ministries. Tim and his team have created dozens and dozens of animated explainer videos about the Bible that have been viewed many millions of times and are being translated into dozens of languages around the world. I've chosen BibleProject videos to go with every chapter of *Becoming God's Family*, and you can access them by scanning the QR codes in the back of this book. Thanks to the vision and generosity of the aging congregation of Central Bible Church, a whole generation is being taught the Scriptures in a way they can understand.

Over ten thousand skaters have come through the doors of SkateChurch over the past thirty years. They skate for an hour, hear a half-hour gospel message, and then skate some more. What started in the basement of CB has become a global movement of churches reaching skateboarders for Christ.

The Spirit of God desires to gather *everyone* to hear and respond to the gospel. With a little vision and a lot of teamwork, we can participate in some of the most exciting work on the planet. An aerial view of the skate warehouse online shows community gardens on one side and more skate ramps on the other. I'm not a bit surprised. If Jeremiah had thought of it, I'm sure he would have included skate ramps alongside the gardens he urged the exiles to plant in Babylon.

DOUBLE VISION

For Daniel, the idea of "seeking the good of the city" while in exile was not an abstract discussion topic. He lived it. Daniel and his friends were among the nobility in Jerusalem selected by the Babylonians for government service. They were taken to Babylon, studied the language of Babylon and its literature, ate at the king's table, and entered the king's service. Working for the good of the city was literally their job.

Daniel has a special knack for understanding dreams and visions, which would have been part of his job description as a court official. After all, the most important source of guidance for ruling the nation comes from the gods by way of dreams and visions.

One night Daniel has a particularly disturbing dream involving beasts that come up out of the sea and a scene that unfolds in the heavens. Before we discuss the details, we need to know what we're reading. The book of Daniel is apocalyptic literature (pronounced *uh-pah-cuh-LIP-tic*). The word *apocalyptic* is from a Greek word that means "unveiling." Apocalyptic literature relies heavily on symbolic representations of political realities. This type of literature was very popular in the centuries leading up to the birth of Jesus, but we don't have an exact equivalent in English. Our closest match is political cartoons.

In a political cartoon, animals stand for countries or for political parties. Colors and other symbols have conventional meanings: Lady Liberty, Uncle Sam, the scales of justice, and so on. If a donkey and an elephant are fighting over the money in a man's pocket, we know the cartoonist is commenting on the problem of high taxation by both Republican and Democratic leaders. The cartoonist does not need to include a key explaining the symbolism because the meanings are widely understood. So too with apocalyptic literature such as the book of Daniel.

As with political cartoons, in apocalyptic literature, animals represent nations. It's common to combine features of more than one animal. Horns symbolize strength and represent kingship. The sea symbolizes the threat of chaos and warfare.

In Daniel's vision of Daniel 7, four beasts come up out of the sea, one after another: a winged lion, a bear with ribs in its mouth, a winged leopard with four heads, and a terrifying beast with iron teeth and ten horns. Confronting these beasts, the Ancient of Days (Yahweh) sits on his flaming throne with robes as white as snow. He strips the beasts of their authority to rule.

Next, Daniel sees "one like a son of man, coming with the clouds of heaven" (Daniel 7:13). The phrase "son of man" is familiar to us because Jesus often uses it to describe himself. It simply means "human." In this case, however, the figure is *like* a son of man. He resembles a human, which is to say he is *not quite* a human. The Ancient of Days gives him everlasting "authority, glory and sovereign power" to rule over all nations (Daniel 7:14).

Daniel isn't sure what to make of all this, so he asks an angel to interpret the vision for him. The explanation goes like this: "The four great beasts are four kings that will rise from the earth. But *the holy people of the Most High* will receive the kingdom and will possess it forever—yes, for ever and ever" (Daniel 7:17-18).

The explanation is puzzling. Did God Almighty give authority to a single figure—"one like a son of man"—or to a group of people— "the holy people of the Most High"? The answer is yes. It's a kind of double vision. The humanlike figure of the vision represents God's holy people. Together, they receive authority and rule on God's behalf.

We dare not miss Jesus' bold claims hundreds of years later when he refers to himself as the "Son of Man." He is not merely being evasive (though he is that, since the religious leaders cannot pin blame on Jesus for claiming to be human). However, by claiming the title "Son of Man," Jesus points to himself as the fulfillment of Daniel's vision. He holds a position of ultimate authority, given from on high (Matthew 9:6; 12:8; 13:41). Jesus says explicitly to his disciples, "The Son of Man is going to come in his Father's glory with his angels, and then he will reward each person according to what they have done" (Matthew 16:27). Jesus claims to be the judge of all (see Matthew 19:28).

Jesus quotes Daniel 7 directly and repeatedly with reference to his own return (Matthew 24:30-31; 25:31; 26:64). After his resurrection, Jesus sends his disciples out to all nations, saying, "All authority in heaven and on earth has been given to me" (Matthew 28:18).

How can the single person of Daniel's vision be a whole group of people? The answer is that Jesus was a representative figure, receiving authority and commissioning the rest of us to act on his behalf. It is on this basis that Paul repeatedly speaks of believers as being "in Christ" (e.g., Romans 8:1; 2 Corinthians 1:21). Paul writes, "We, though many, form one body, and each member belongs to all the others" (Romans 12:5). He says again, "In Christ Jesus you are all sons of God through faith. For all of you who were baptized into

Christ have clothed yourselves with Christ. There is neither Jew nor Greek, there is neither slave nor free, there is neither male nor female—for all of you are one in Christ Jesus" (Galatians 3:26-28 NET). It only works if we come together as one. We must be so radically committed to the will of the Father, so loyal to his rule, that we lay aside our own ambitions and devote ourselves fully to his. The rule of the Father expressed in his Son will then be ours to share. Together.

Speaking of working together, Daniel was not the only Jew who served the pagan empire, and his approach to that work was not the only model for God's people. Daniel apparently kept his Jewish name, and his devotion to Yahweh was public knowledge. (Yes, Nebuchadnezzar gave him a new name, but no one, not even the king or his mother, seems to have used it much.) It was no secret to anyone that Daniel was Jewish. Daniel lived through the end of the Babylonian kingdom and the rise of the Persian Empire, retaining his position in the government to serve rulers of both empires.

Esther's story is dramatically different. Summoned to the palace in Persia without her consent, Esther is destined for the king's bedroom. She conceals her identity as a Jew by using her Persian name and by doing whatever she is told. Unlike Daniel, she does not refuse to eat the king's food. Sometimes Bible readers criticize Esther for capitulating to ungodly behavior. Wasn't she breaking Jewish law?

Esther conceals her identity as a matter of survival. When the time is right—after Haman makes plans to exterminate the Jewish people and her uncle Mordecai urges her to act—she lays all her cards on the table for the sake of others. Esther's ultimate loyalty is not to the king or to her own career path but to her people. She leverages her power to expose Haman's plot. Esther's uncle Mordecai rises to second in rank to the king, esteemed "because he worked for the good of his people and spoke up for the welfare of all the Jews" (Esther 10:3).

Daniel works for the good of his city while publicly maintaining his Jewish identity. So does Mordecai. Esther works for the good of God's people by blending in and waiting. Together, they offer two models for navigating the life of faith in a pagan empire.

THE TEMPLE THAT WON'T BE BUILT

Unlike Daniel and Esther, who rose to prominence in the courts of foreign kings during the exile, the prophet Ezekiel lived among the common people. He too went with the people of Judah into exile and lived in Babylon. The assignments God gave Ezekiel were the most unusual of all. Many of his messages came in the form of street theater. Ezekiel ate a scroll, laid siege to a clay tablet in the street, baked bread over cow dung while lying on his side, shaved his head with a sword and did odd things with his hair, and dug through the mudbrick walls of his house.

Two features of Ezekiel's messages are pertinent to the theme we are tracing of God's presence in the community. First, God gives Ezekiel a vision in Ezekiel 1 that sets him stammering. Standing on banks of the river in Babylon where the Judean exiles settled, Ezekiel sees a vision of the throne of Yahweh flanked by four bizarre creatures. Each has four wings and four faces: a human, a lion, an ox, and an eagle. Their movements are reminiscent of lightning flashing back and forth. Yahweh's throne is on a pavement of precious stones carried by intersecting wheels, moving up, down, back, and forth without turning. On the throne is a glowing figure emanating brilliant light.

This striking vision is proof that Yahweh has not abandoned his people. His glory shows up among the exiles in Babylon. The vision also makes clear that the Babylonians have not captured Yahweh. He moves about freely. His glory cannot be contained. For a nation whose worship of Yahweh had centered on the temple in Jerusalem—which now lay in ruins—this would have been deeply encouraging.

Twenty years later, God gives Ezekiel another vision, transporting him back to Jerusalem, where he encounters an angel with a measuring stick in his hand. Ezekiel follows the angel as he measures the temple in his vision. It is not the actual temple, because the dimensions are square instead of rectangular. It is not the blueprints of a temple to be built after the exile either, because the angel measures only the length and width of the area, not the height. That missing dimension would make the new temple impossible to build.[5]

The description of Ezekiel's temple tour lasts several chapters. The most important moment in the vision is when "the glory of the God of Israel" comes from the east, enters the eastern gate, and fills the temple (Ezekiel 43:1-5). Ezekiel recognizes immediately that this is the same divine presence he saw in his opening vision in Ezekiel 1. Of his own free will, Yahweh has returned to take up residence again in the temple of Ezekiel's vision.

Certain furnishings and people are missing from the temple vision. The angel speaks of the kings who have defiled the temple and says they will be no more. Instead, he refers to the human ruler of Israel as a "prince"—his way of demoting Israel's rulers because Yahweh alone would be king (Ezekiel 44:3). The high priest is notably absent from the vision as well. Given Judah's history of corrupted worship, the high priest has been deposed, along with the furnishings unique to high-priestly service, such as the ark of the covenant. Only the priests who descended from Zadok were to carry out sacrifices on the altar, because they remained faithful to the covenant when other priestly families did not (Ezekiel 44:15-16). Zadok was priest during David's reign; he was loyal to David during his sons' insurrections by supporting Solomon as the rightful successor to the throne (2 Samuel 15:24-29; 1 Kings 1:8).

God's vision for Ezekiel then expands out beyond the temple to the land itself, dividing it anew for the twelve tribes. The land redistribution functions as a reset button. The exile has disrupted Israel's land inheritance. Following the exile, new boundaries will determine where they settle. Remarkably, this time land will also be allotted to foreigners who have made their home among the Israelites (Ezekiel 47:22-23). They will join a tribe and finally belong. God's plan for the restoration of his presence and people in the land includes a permanent place for foreigners.

Ezekiel's message to the people calls them to repent of their sins and follow God's regulations. Another powerful aspect of the vision is a freshwater river, flowing from under the threshold of the temple eastward and into the Dead Sea (Ezekiel 47). The river grows deeper the farther it flows and brings life wherever it goes. Fruit trees line its banks, and fish swim in it. Remarkably, it makes saltwater fresh. Even the Dead Sea, where nothing lives (even bacteria!) because of the high mineral content of the water, becomes a fisherman's paradise.

> God's plan for the restoration of his presence and people in the land includes a permanent place for foreigners.

The river is our clearest indication that the vision is symbolic rather than a blueprint for temple rebuilding. It defies the laws of nature by growing as it flows and by transforming saltwater into freshwater. The point of the vision is to reawaken hope for the return of God's presence and abundant blessing to the land of Israel. The book ends with this treasured confidence: "And the name of the city from that time on will be: YAHWEH IS THERE" (Ezekiel 48:35).

The realization of Ezekiel's vision depends on the will of the people to be regathered under new terms. They cannot keep living as they have been and expect God's presence to return. They cannot go their own way and expect God's blessing. They will have to release their stubborn hold on the past and make space for new neighbors.

A student of mine in Canada was ordained by his denomination and assigned a dying church. They had a building but only a handful of members and no money to speak of. Dylan prayed, "Lord, you've given us a building. Show us how you want us to use it to serve this community." The area around the church included many people struggling to make ends meet. Dylan registered to receive overstocked or damaged goods from Amazon to share with neighbors in need. People began to come. Then he started a food pantry. He's still early in the process of revitalizing this church, but already he's brimming with stories of answered prayers and met needs.

An unchurched neighbor asked, "You don't happen to have a ceiling fan, do you? We need one." Dylan checked the Amazon shipment that had come after midnight. A ceiling fan was right on top of the pile, with exactly the right specifications. Neighbors who have never darkened the door of a church are coming, joining the Bible study, and beginning to serve. As they gather, the Spirit is hovering, doing his work, and lives are being changed.

Dylan is experiencing the presence of God as he participates in God's work in his community. By welcoming and serving their neighbors, Dylan's fledgling community is being rebuilt into a temple for the Spirit. The most pressing need is not each person's independence but rather belonging. When we work together for the good of our cities, new communities of faith can emerge that begin to act like family and experience the presence of God together.

KEY IDEAS

- The Old Testament prophets cast a vision for God's people of deep interdependence on God and one another.
- Jeremiah urged the exiles to invest in the prosperity of their neighborhoods, creating space for *everyone* to gather and find a place to belong.

- Loyalty to God's rule requires us to lay aside our own ambitions and leverage whatever power we have on behalf of others.
- Ezekiel's vision of God's presence in the restored community required the people to make room for new neighbors.

DIGGING DEEPER

Daniel Block. *Ezekiel.* 2 vols. New International Commentary on the Old Testament. Eerdmans, 1997.

Jonathan Brooks. *Church Forsaken: Practicing Presence in Neglected Neighborhoods.* InterVarsity Press, 2018.

Aaron Chalmers. *Interpreting the Prophets: Reading, Understanding and Preaching from the Worlds of the Prophets.* IVP Academic, 2015.

Michael J. Rhodes. *Just Discipleship: Biblical Justice in an Unjust World.* IVP Academic, 2023.

Related videos from BibleProject: "Apocalyptic Literature," "Gospel of the Kingdom," and "The Way of the Exile."

6

PROCESSING FAMILY TRAUMA

COLLECTIVE TEARS

Once, while waiting for a connecting flight in the Dallas airport, I saw a little boy traveling with his grandmother. He was video chatting with his mother while waiting at the gate. He was probably two years old and was obviously delighted to be with his mother, even though she was on screen rather than in person. He simply could not contain his joy and kept turning the phone around to show the rest of us in the waiting area so that we could see her and be happy too. His language skills had not developed yet, but he clearly wanted all of us to know that he had the most important person in the world on the phone!

Shared attention is a human value that adds meaning to our lives. It's not enough to hear good news. We want to share it. Similarly, secret sorrows are twice as heavy. It makes a world of difference when someone shares in our pain.

One of the most distinctive stages of human infant development is the development of shared attention. Babies learn to point at a very young age. They find pleasure in following our gaze to the same object.[1]

Shared attention is also one of the great losses of our generation. During my childhood as well as when my kids were little, families used to read aloud together, gather around the radio to listen to the same program, or meet in the family room to watch the same TV show. Now it is increasingly common for each member of the same household to stare at their own screen, scrolling on their phone or working on their laptop, or watching TV with headphones. Our attention has splintered so that we're no longer looking at and thinking about the same thing.

In 2002, my mom was in an auto accident that left her with a brain injury. Lights and sounds and movement and smells all overwhelmed her neurological system to the extent that she could not safely attend church. For over a decade, she and my dad watched a church service online. Their favorite one was out of state. Although they had a chance to visit that church once or twice in person, it was difficult to cultivate a robust sense of belonging to an out-of-state congregation. They felt like they got to know those on camera, but nobody saw my parents. Watching online was better than nothing, but it was not ideal. Mom is much healthier now and able to attend church in person. It's made all the difference for both of my parents to participate again in embodied community with other believers. Nothing can truly substitute for the life and friendships made possible by local gatherings. For those unable to attend church services, local congregations can find ways to stay connected through midweek Bible studies, home visits, phone calls, and care packages.

When we gather for worship, among the many other things we're doing, we are cultivating shared attention. Watching a church service on demand from the comforts of my own home can never quite accomplish that. For some it may be necessary for a season due to health constraints or work schedules, but the ideal is to be physically present with one another. Whenever possible, we should gather in person. Humans share a fundamental need for an embodied community. This is why solitary confinement is an effective form of punishment. We are meant to be built *together* into a dwelling place of God by the Spirit.

The book of Psalms recognizes the value of corporate worship. It is not simply a collection of individual prayers. Many psalms employ *we* and *us*, rather than *I* and *me*, meant to be prayed or sung by groups of people. Gathering for corporate worship decenters *my* schedule and *my* preferences. Even the individual prayers that appear in the collection are offered for the use and benefit of the whole community. To sing or pray them together cultivates shared attention to collective joys and sorrows. It builds solidarity and fosters unity.

> When we gather for worship, we are cultivating shared attention.

Suffering is far worse when we feel alone in it. That fact motivates the psalmist to call for God to pay attention. "Awake, Lord! Why do you sleep? Rouse yourself! Do not reject us forever. Why do you hide your face and forget our misery and oppression?" (Psalm 44:23-24). It's not just one psalm that is this honest. I count seventeen psalms that wonder why God has rejected or forgotten or become angry with his people (Psalms 6; 13; 27; 42–44; 60; 74; 77–78; 85; 88–90; 95; 106; 108). Many other psalms wrestle with human foes, calling on God to rescue his people from false accusation or undue harm. In fact, lament psalms account for over 40 percent of the book of Psalms.

> O God, why have you rejected us forever?
>   Why does your anger smolder against the sheep of
>   your pasture?

Remember the nation you purchased long ago,
    The people of your inheritance, whom you redeemed—
    Mount Zion, where you dwelt.
Turn your steps toward these everlasting ruins,
    All this destruction the enemy has brought on the
        sanctuary. (Psalm 74:1-3)

To pray or sing these prayers together opens space for honesty. Failure to do so can unwittingly result in gatherings where people don't feel free to express their pain.

A friend of mine suffers from infertility. For over twenty years, she and her husband have hoped and prayed for children but never conceived. She told me once about a small group she attended. The women were taking turns sharing prayer requests. That day, my friend couldn't hold it in any longer. She vented her frustration over their long years of waiting and trying and facing disappointment month after month. The women sat in awkward silence, not knowing how to respond, and my friend decided never to open up again in that context about her grief.

Considering the Psalms, my friend's spoken sorrow was fully appropriate, but her church family was not well versed in the language of lament. When we learn to pray our pain honestly and to appropriately receive others' pain, we become communities that can more effectively share one another's burdens.

> When we learn to pray our pain honestly and to appropriately receive others' pain, we become communities that can more effectively share one another's burdens.

O God, do not remain silent;
    do not turn a deaf ear,
    do not stand aloof, O God.

See how your enemies growl,
>   how your foes rear their heads.
With cunning they conspire against your people;
>   they plot against those you cherish.
"Come," they say, "let us destroy them as a nation,
>   so that Israel's name is remembered no more."
>   (Psalm 83:1-4)

Honest prayer in community cultivates a clear-eyed vision for all of us of where we stand, what we need, and to whom we must look for deliverance.

WHY IS GOD SO ANGRY?

The prophets do not chase down individuals, chiding them for their personal sin. The prophet Isaiah is not on the lookout for bad apples. He and other prophets address the nation as a whole: "Woe to the sinful nation, a people whose guilt is great, a brood of evildoers, children given to corruption!" (Isaiah 1:4). Together, the nation of Judah has become a place where wickedness is the norm. The social elites tolerate drunkenness, greed, and violence. Isaiah proclaims,

> Woe to those who make unjust laws,
>   to those who issue oppressive decrees,
> to deprive the poor of their rights
>   and withhold justice from the oppressed of
>   my people,
> making widows their prey
>   and robbing the fatherless.
> What will you do on the day of reckoning,
>   when disaster comes from afar? (Isaiah 10:1-3)

Many people today struggle with the violence of God in the Old Testament prophets. Divine vengeance can be difficult to stomach. That's why it's so important for us to notice *why* God is angry. Yahweh's wrath is uniformly directed at those who mistreat the vulnerable. In the passage above, the prophet draws attention to the fate of the poor, the oppressed, the widows, and the fatherless. Another category of society's most vulnerable are immigrants, who lack land of their own and the benefits that come with full citizenship. The prophet announces,

> Strengthen the feeble hands,
>   steady the knees that give way;
> say to those with fearful hearts,
>   "Be strong, do not fear;
> your God will come,
>   he will come with vengeance;
> with divine retribution
>   he will come to save you."
> Then will the eyes of the blind be opened
>   and the ears of the deaf unstopped.
> Then will the lame leap like a deer,
>   and the mute tongue shout for joy. (Isaiah 35:3-6)

Yahweh's punishment serves to liberate and provide for those on the margins. His anger is aimed at those who exploit, which directly benefits the weak, the anxious, and those with disabilities, who are on the receiving end of oppression.

I suspect that many of us think of sin and salvation as a personal issue: *As an individual, I make a bad choice to disobey God. God allows Jesus to take the punishment I deserve so I personally can be free to live with him forever.*

This version of the gospel message would have sounded very flat to the prophet Isaiah. For him, society was rotten through and through and in need of massive renovation. The whole system was built to allow wickedness to go unchecked. Collective failures to follow God required group consequences and a new vision of what they could become with the transformative presence of God in their midst. The prophet's ultimate vision was not just for individuals to return home to Judah but to gather the nations around the presence of God at the temple to establish a multiethnic family, which would form the center of a city and nation marked by justice and peace.

THE TRAUMA THAT MAKES US WHO WE ARE

The claymation movie *Chicken Run* (DreamWorks, 2000) features a visionary chicken named Ginger who works tirelessly to free all the chickens from an English farm ruled by the tyrannical Mrs. Tweedy. It's clear that Ginger can leave the farm at will any time. She has successfully escaped using every method imaginable—tunneling under the fence, becoming a stowaway, launching herself over the fence, and donning disguises. But Ginger won't leave without *all* the chickens. Finding a way for one chicken to escape is easy. Finding a way to get hundreds of chickens out of the farm all at once seems impossible, especially when most are content to stay put.

One day, a new rooster shows up on the farm, an American named Rocky who escaped from the circus. Rocky is a player. He's used to being independent, unencumbered by relational ties. Ginger is under the misimpression that Rocky knows how to fly. She imagines he can help them escape the farm by teaching them all to fly, so she pressures him into it. Rocky plays along for a while because he likes all the female attention and because he needs their help hiding from the circus master.

Since Rocky has never flown and has no idea how, his efforts are one big and entirely selfish bluff. To be blunt, he doesn't care about anyone but himself. Rocky thinks Ginger is wound way too tightly. He calls her "hard-boiled" and "intense," urging her to relax and tone down her message.

For Ginger, truth telling is indispensable. She repeatedly brings to everyone's attention that their lives are in utter danger. Any hen who does not lay an egg for several days in a row could end up on Mrs. Tweedy's dinner table. Ginger is convinced that a better life awaits them beyond the barbed-wire fences where the grass is green and no farmer monitors their production. To get them there, Ginger understands the need to foster discontentment by unveiling the dangers around them.

Her tireless work on behalf of the community already makes this story a compelling example for a book on the church, but it's her leadership in identity formation that I find especially intriguing. Ginger knows that if the other hens are content with the status quo, they lack the will to do the hard work required to escape. When Mrs. Tweedy launches a new business strategy—selling chicken pies— Ginger realizes they have no time to lose. She confronts the community with the hard facts: if they don't escape immediately, their lives will end abruptly, wrapped in pastry crust.

Ginger reminds me of the biblical poets. Aside from the Psalms, we can read the prophets' unflinching assessment of their national predicament as well as the abject grief in the book of Lamentations. The subject matter of these books is often ominous. Rocky would have urged them to lighten up. These lyrics linger on some of the most troubling chapters in Israel's history, recalling the devastation of the attacks of the Assyrians and Babylonians, the destruction of Jerusalem, and the despondency of exile.

How deserted lies the city,
    once so full of people!
How like a widow is she,
    who once was great among the nations!
She who was queen among the provinces
    has now become a slave. (Lamentations 1:1)

My eyes fail from weeping,
   I am in torment within;
My heart is poured out on the ground
   because my people are destroyed,
Because children and infants faint
   in the streets of the city. (Lamentations 2:11)

Remember, LORD, what has happened to us;
   look, and see our disgrace.
Our inheritance has been turned over to strangers,
   our homes to foreigners.
We have become fatherless,
   our mothers are widows. (Lamentations 5:1-2)

Lament continues to fuel Israel's prayers long after they return to their land. Songs of sorrow mark the community, keeping alive vivid memories of those harrowing years. The book of Lamentations is still read aloud every year by Jewish communities on the ninth day of the Hebrew month of Av, which commemorates the destruction of the temple—first by the Babylonians in 586 BCE and then by the Romans in 70 CE.

They say that those who do not know their history are doomed to repeat it. Sometimes our poets are best at recognizing the danger of the status quo. Without those traumatic memories of losing the land, God's people stand in danger of losing it again. Any community asleep at the wheel will crash and burn. Collective identity is not a self-driving car.

One danger for the church is when we fail to attend to the tragedies of others we don't see as part of our tribe. The New Testament insists that God is making us into *one* people in Christ. That process involves—even *requires*—that we begin to understand that tragedies affecting other believers and even nonbelievers are *our* tragedies, whether we worship in the same building or not. The human family is our family; some members may be estranged, but ultimately all belong. The plight of Ukrainian churches under attack is *our* plight. The harrowing losses of life in Gaza and Israel are *our* losses. The attempted extermination of the Uyghur people in China is *our* predicament. Persecution and discrimination, violence and poverty, government unrest and natural disasters—anything affecting the human family is ours to lament.

The escape from Tweedy's farm would not have been possible without a collective sense of urgency about the danger of staying and without the solidarity of the lone ranger rooster from the land of the free and the home of the brave. After Ginger discovers the awful truth that Rocky doesn't know how to fly, he slips away from the farm. His charade is over. Rocky tries to move on but discovers that he has begun to care about the plight of the other chickens. Thoughts of their fate compel him to turn around and rejoin their rebellion. Empathy makes all the difference.

With apologies for spoiling the movie for you (I'll let the movie surprise you with *how*), Ginger and the chickens eventually escape with a little help from Rocky. But in their new home on the banks of a river under the shade of giant trees, the green grass does not lull them into complacency. New chicks attend classes in which they learn their history and the story of their great escape. They must understand where they've come from to prevent the possibility of re-enslavement. Without shared memories of their collective trauma, they would become vulnerable.

Most of us probably imagine we'd be better off forgetting our traumas. But the historic community of faith has understood how essential trauma is for our survival. It makes us who we are.

UNDERSTANDING TRAUMA

These days, it seems everybody is talking about trauma or PTSD (posttraumatic stress disorder), but many of us do so without understanding what qualifies as trauma and why it affects us so much. The word *trauma* is not new, but its usage is on the rise over the past fifty years. Trauma refers to the result of a distressing event—not the event itself but what it does to us. Two people can witness the same event; one carries on as usual, and the other is shattered by it. The difference depends on how the incident affects our ways of seeing and understanding the world.

As Old Testament scholar Michelle Keener explains, "Trauma shakes and breaks the fundamental beliefs that make up our worldview."[a] The reason we experience an event as traumatic is that it violates our sense of how things work, or ought to work, in the world. We don't have a grid for it or a place to file away what happened. A key part of the healing process is developing a trauma narrative that incorporates what happened into our larger life story.[b]

This is what the biblical writers do as they narrate some of Israel's most traumatic events. *How could the Levite surrender his concubine to a crowd of violent men driven by lust in Judges 19-20?* This is the kind of thing that happens when everyone does what is right in their own eyes. *How could God's people lose the Promised Land and get dragged off into exile?* This can happen when God's people are unfaithful to the covenant they made with Yahweh.

Why would a righteous man like Job experience devastating loss? One reason the dialogue in Job goes on for so long is that each character tries to force Job's experience to fit his way of seeing the world. In the end, Job recognizes God's sovereignty in a way that allows him to let go of his need to understand why he suffered. The trauma narrative that emerges allows room for mystery, and he is finally able to move on.

Our world today is riddled with fresh communal traumas: wars that drag on for months over disputed land, terrorist attacks, mass shootings, violent protests, death without trial at the hands of law enforcement, clergy abuse, and the refusal of some churches to support victims well. Some of us may think that the best way forward is whatever will help us forget these tragedies quickly. However, healing comes not when we bury our collective traumas but when we look them full in the face, mourn them, and find ways to integrate them into our stories and our shared life.

Our children need to know about the challenges we've faced and how God helped us to overcome them. Remembering trauma reminds us that we are shaped by what has happened to us and also that we have moved on and found life and hope again. Knowing that can help our communities face fresh wounds with courage.

DEFIANT PRAISE

Lament is not the only glue that forges bonds between community members. For ancient Israel, praise psalms also play a key role in maintaining national identity.[2] When we stop to consider what praise entails, we discover that praise makes the most daring political claims of all. Praise psalms do not simply state the obvious; while exalting Yahweh, they simultaneously demote every possible rival.[3] As Walter Brueggemann puts it, "Hymns of praise are acts of devotion with political and polemical overtones . . . [and] acts of defiance of the world that is in front of us."[4] Psalms of praise may seem positive, but each claim implies an emphatic negative: *Yahweh* is Lord! Therefore, Marduk is not! These psalms have the audacity to articulate an unseen reality in which the so-called powers of this world are revealed to be nothing more than pawns.

Two factors prevent us from seeing this. First, our English translations render the unique divine name, Yahweh, as LORD (in small caps). In an attempt to honor God's name, we have erased it. *Lord* is not a name; it's a title indicating a person of status. "Praise the Lord" sounds generic, like a canned message on a store-bought card. "Praise Yahweh" is specific and therefore bold. A second factor that inhibits some of us from appreciating the power of praise psalms is being raised in monotheistic contexts. Our parents and teachers dutifully told us there was only one God. In that context, praise seems practically unnecessary.

Israel's psalms are far grittier than we realize. The people of Israel live in a world crowded with possible deities to worship. Several thick books on my office shelves catalog these gods alphabetically, explaining what each one was known for. Re, Isis, Hathor, and Osiris in Egypt, among dozens of others. Baal, Asherah, El, and Dagon in Canaan. Marduk, Isis, Ashur, Enlil, Ea, Tiamat, and Adad in Mesopotamia, to name a few. Every time the covenant community recites a psalm, they are making a claim for Yahweh and against other gods.

For these ancient cultures, worship is a matter of national security. They believe that the gods are responsible for the success of their crops, the survival of their children, and the outcomes of their battles. Kings rule under divine patronage. The task of royalty is to do the bidding of the gods and maintain order in their realm. Most gods in the ancient Near East are thought to have a particular specialty and a specific jurisdiction.

When we read the praise psalms against that backdrop, a whole new world opens to us—a world with the potential of reshaping our own. Let's consider Psalm 96 as an example. We'll walk through it and notice what it says to a people in a polytheistic world.[5]

Sing to Yahweh a new song;
  sing to Yahweh, all the earth.

Sing to Yahweh, praise his name;
> proclaim his salvation day after day.

Declare his glory among the nations,
> his marvelous deeds among all peoples. (Psalm 96:1-3)

Psalm 96 is not generic. It cannot be used in just any worship context but only to worship Yahweh, the God of Israel. That's what makes this psalm so radical: "all the earth" must praise Yahweh, not just Israelites. All must hear the story of "his salvation."

For Israel, Yahweh's salvation is not a future hope but something they had already experienced when Yahweh defeated Pharaoh at the sea. Yahweh's salvation offered much more than an individual sense of reassurance. It entailed the decisive defeat of Egypt and its gods (Exodus 12:12; 15:2).

For great is Yahweh and most worthy of praise;
> he is to be feared above all gods.

For all the gods of the nations are idols,
> but Yahweh made the heavens.

Splendor and majesty are before him;
> strength and glory are in his sanctuary. (Psalm 96:4-6)

The insult of this psalm is deliberate and obvious, once you look for it. To exalt Yahweh is to demote any rivals. Yahweh has all the splendor, while the gods of the nations are nothing more than mute objects. To sing this denies the validity of the foundation myths of all of Israel's neighbors.

Ascribe to Yahweh, all you families of nations,
> ascribe to Yahweh glory and strength.

Ascribe to Yahweh the glory due his name;
> bring an offering and come into his courts.

Worship Yahweh in the splendor of his holiness;
> tremble before him, all the earth. (Psalm 96:7-9)

What's remarkable about these verses is their call for the nations to worship at the temple in Jerusalem. It's not enough for other nations to admit Yahweh's power from afar. Their acknowledgment must translate into action of the most humbling variety—a pilgrimage to Yahweh's own temple in Jerusalem, where they bring tribute and bow before him.

> Say among the nations, "Yahweh reigns."
>> The world is firmly established, it cannot be moved;
>> He will judge the peoples with equity. (Psalm 96:10)

To say that Yahweh reigns not only undermines the authority of every other god in the ancient pantheons of Israel's neighbors, but it also calls into question the legitimacy of every human monarch other than the one Yahweh anointed. No king rules except by divine appointment. One of a king's first priorities is to establish the legitimacy of his rule by proving that the gods have selected him. If those gods are unseated from their heavenly thrones, then the king is himself illegitimate. These are fighting words.

> Let the heavens rejoice, let the earth be glad;
>> let the sea resound, and all that is in it.
> Let the fields be jubilant, and everything in them;
>> let all the trees of the forest sing for joy.
> Let all creation rejoice before Yahweh, for he comes,
>> he comes to judge the earth.
> He will judge the world in righteousness
>> and the peoples in his faithfulness. (Psalm 96:11-13)

Israel's neighbors depict their gods using the symbols of animals and see divine symbolism in trees and oceans. In contrast, Psalm 96 portrays every created thing celebrating Yahweh's rule and standing before him as the ultimate judge.

Praise is what unites and makes possible the radical transformation God has in mind for us. It inaugurates a new kind of community under the rule of our gracious King. According to Psalm 96, this new community will be global in its scope, so long as everyone recognizes Yahweh's supreme rule. At the end of the day, all will answer to Yahweh.

> Praise is what unites and makes possible the radical transformation God has in mind for us.

CONTEXT IS EVERYTHING

The 1965 film *The Sound of Music* offers an analogy to illustrate the audacity of praise psalms.[6] Captain von Trapp is a retired naval officer in Austria raising his seven children with the help of one governess after another. The children are hard on these substitute mothers, so the captain turns to a nearby abbey for help—maybe a nun can keep his children in line. The abbey sends Fräulein Maria, who wins the hearts of the children as well as their father.

Their romance is set against the backdrop of a growing threat of occupation by Nazi Germany in 1938. The captain and Maria return home from their honeymoon to find a Nazi flag flying over their front door, a summons by telegram to serve in Hitler's navy, and an invitation to perform as a family in the Salzburg Music Festival. They attempt to escape to Switzerland with their children that very night under the cover of darkness but are caught in the act by Nazi soldiers. Thinking quickly, the family pretends they are heading to perform in the music festival instead.

The joyous evening of music is strained by the presence of Nazis guarding the exits. In the front row sits the Nazi officer ready to escort Captain von Trapp to his new post in Hitler's navy. While the judges evaluate the results of the competition, Captain von Trapp regales the waiting crowd with a final song. Alone in the spotlight, he sings "Edelweiss," a simple song about a white alpine flower native to Austria. The lyrics are not in themselves seditious, but the song functions as an unofficial national anthem. Sung in this context, the captain's audacity is plain. The lilting melody nourishes the crowd's longing for Austrian independence. The captain is overcome with emotion, unable to finish the song. Maria, the children, and the entire audience join him for the finish, ending with the hopeful plea, "Bless my homeland forever!"

Praise psalms are like this. On their own, they don't strike us as rebellious, but set against the backdrop of Assyrian or Persian rule, they are a form of insurrection. Psalms of praise exalt Yahweh above all human rulers and rival gods, diminishing their claim to power.

By doing so, they form an alternative community, gathered around the praise of Yahweh. What happens to these psalms when we sing them in *our* context?

By personally praying psalms of praise and lament from the Bible, we develop the habit of bringing our deepest needs to God and of celebrating his work in our lives. The Psalms shape our capacity to pray by providing model prayers with both depth of feeling and breadth of topic. That prepares us for more robust and faithful forms of corporate worship. The Psalms enlarge our capacity to receive the pains and joys of others and walk alongside them without feeling the need to fix them.

When we sing together about Yahweh's kingship during an election year, we're reminded that our ultimate hope is in God, not our national government or local leaders. When we offer thanks to God for what he has done on our behalf, our posture shifts away from self-congratulation or self-aggrandizement toward gratitude and humility.

Some Christians in our world today live under the constant scrutiny of federal surveillance. If they are caught gathering with fellow Christians to sing praise to God, they could face frightening consequences. These brothers and sisters know well the political implications of praise.

In other contexts, praise of God has been tightly knit with allegiance to a certain political party. Over time, as the lines between party platform and biblical teaching become blurred, the distinction fades between the King of all and human leaders. In times like these, we need praise psalms to remind us that Yahweh will not tolerate the worship of anyone or anything else. He is bound to no human agenda and refuses to guarantee the rulership of any mortal government that does not exalt him as supreme.

THE PROBLEM WITH CHRISTIAN NATIONALISM

Conversations about Christian nationalism can become very heated, in part because people understand the label in different ways. Some equate it with positive values such as civic engagement or patriotism, while others associate it with anti-immigrant sentiments or even a call to take up arms against the government and take it back for God.

I'm reserving the label "Christian nationalist" for those who believe that their country was uniquely chosen by God for a special purpose in the world and that it can fulfill that purpose only if its elected officials "recognize Christianity as the official religion," "promote and enforce Christian values," and advance the gospel.[a] One common attribute of Christian nationalists in the United States is the sense of being a persecuted minority.

Christian nationalists often push for greater rights and freedoms and oppose any perceived loss of social influence. As Russell Moore explains, "Christian nationalism is not a politically enthusiastic version of Christianity, nor is it a religiously informed patriotism. Christian nationalism is a prosperity gospel for nation-states, a liberation theology for white people."[b] However, the United States is not the only country with a strong and growing Christian nationalist movement. Nagaland in India is another example. Many Naga Christians believe that as a nation they have a special role to play in God's kingdom.[c] The church in Brazil is also strongly nationalistic. Throughout Latin America, evangelicals are making strides in public influence, and the ideas of Christian nationalism are taking root. Even Zionism is another form of nationalism that often fails to account for the differences between ancient Israel, which entered a covenant with Yahweh and agreed to live by his commands, and the modern-day secular state of Israel, which has developed a different set of priorities and commitments. Sometimes Christians assume that because modern Israel shares the same name as ancient Israel, we cannot critique its policies. The reality is more complex than that.

Caleb Campbell is a pastor in Arizona. He was increasingly distressed by the way his community was being torn apart by political disagreements. Members of his congregation had been swept up in a political movement that seemed to be fueled by fear and anxiety. At one point he listed three hundred people he knew whose relationships had fractured over these issues. After many months of frustration, Caleb realized he needed to better understand Christian nationalism so that he could more effectively disciple his congregation.

To this end, Caleb began attending Christian nationalist events, receiving their newsletters, and conversing with his neighbors. His mission was to understand what hopes and fears motivated Christian nationalists. Caleb's book *Disarming Leviathan* is based on that journey of seeking to bring the claims of the gospel to bear on his ministry context.

Christian nationalism tends to be self-centered. As Dominique Gilliard explains, "Citizenship grants power, and how we use this power bears witness to where our allegiance lies. Kingdom citizens sacrificially use their [earthly] citizenship to seek the peace and prosperity of their communities, to expose and address systemic sin, as well as to care for and dignify the least of these."[d]

When Jesus' followers were a struggling minority under the thumb of Rome, God did not urge them to take up arms or seize power so that God's kingdom purposes could be carried out. Instead, he told them to "take up their cross," to serve selflessly, and to endure persecution. Although this does not preclude an active involvement in the democratic process, Jesus' followers did not have this option in the Roman Empire, and we can learn from their posture. We must not confuse our votes, our lobbies, and our proposed legislation with the establishment of God's kingdom, which does not depend on any human government.

A true grasp of the doctrine of the family of God sucks the wind out of Christian nationalism because it recognizes that our truest identity and most fervent hope is not found in our nation but in our church family. Every time we pray the Lord's Prayer—"Your kingdom come, your will be done"—we're praying for the end of America and every other national entity on earth.[e] God's kingdom is the only one that will last.

KEY IDEAS

- Humans share a fundamental need for an embodied faith community that gives shared attention to the presence of God.

- Honest prayer in community cultivates healthy dependence on God.

- The vision of the Old Testament prophets was to gather the nations around the presence of Yahweh to establish a multiethnic family marked by justice and peace.

- Those who forget their history are doomed to repeat it. Biblical lament reminds God's people of their painful past and galvanizes them to live faithfully in the present.

- Biblical praise exalts Yahweh above every potential rival. The exclusivity of Israel's praise inaugurates a new king of community under the rule of our gracious King.

DIGGING DEEPER

Caleb Campbell. *Disarming Leviathan: Loving Your Christian Nationalist Neighbor.* IVP Academic, 2024.

Michael Card. *A Sacred Sorrow: Reaching Out to God in the Lost Language of Lament.* NavPress, 2005.

Dominique Dubois Gilliard. *Subversive Witness: Scripture's Call to Leverage Privilege.* Zondervan, 2021.

Emmanuel Katongole. *Born from Lament: The Theology and Politics of Hope in Africa.* Eerdmans, 2017.

Michelle Keener. *Comfort in the Ashes: Explorations in the Book of Job to Support Trauma Survivors.* InterVarsity Press, 2025.

Kyle Strobel and Jamin Goggin. *The Way of the Dragon or the Way of the Lamb: Searching for Jesus' Path of Power in a Church That Has Abandoned It.* Thomas Nelson, 2021.

Related videos from BibleProject: "Psalms," "The Book of Psalms," and "Lamentations."

7

FAMILY DRAMA

CIRCLE THE WAGONS

Zerubbabel, Ezra, and Nehemiah lived at the tail end of the period of Judah's exile in Babylon. They were among the initial waves of those who returned to Judah to rebuild the temple and the community. Since those are the key themes we're following in this book, let's take a closer look at what we can learn from them. Although these men are often celebrated as biblical heroes, a closer read of these books offers a more complicated portrait. While Nehemiah successfully rebuilds the wall around Jerusalem and Ezra calls the community to prioritize worship, Ezra and Nehemiah's selective reading of the Torah results in unnecessarily harsh reforms.

The returnees face enormous challenges. Because of Nebuchadnezzar's attack on Jerusalem many years earlier, Jerusalem's walls and its most important building—the temple—are decimated. Imagine rebuilding a city from the rubble with no Home Depot and no Walmart nearby. Everyone needs to find and rebuild places to live, meanwhile expending the enormous energy required to keep food on the table and make progress on rebuilding walls and restoring

streets. Zerubbabel is among the first wave of returnees. He attempts
to rebuild the temple. Some of the non-Jewish residents of the land
approach him with an offer to help. Instead of welcoming their collaboration, Zerubbabel rejects them: "You have no part with us in
building a temple to our God. We alone will build it for the LORD,
the God of Israel, as King Cyrus, the king of Persia, commanded us"
(Ezra 4:3). His lack of imagination is disappointing. It doesn't seem
like he's been listening to the prophets.

At that time, Zechariah the prophet is living in Jerusalem (Ezra 5:1;
6:14). Through him, Yahweh reveals a vision much grander than
Zerubbabel's:

> "Shout and be glad, Daughter Zion. For I am coming, and I will
> live among you," declares the LORD. "*Many nations will be joined
> with the LORD in that day and will become my people.* I will live
> among you and you will know that the LORD Almighty has
> sent me to you. The LORD will inherit Judah as his portion in
> the holy land and will again choose Jerusalem." (Zecha-
> riah 2:10-12, emphasis added)

The book of Isaiah also announces, "Foreigners will rebuild your
walls" (Isaiah 60:10). If God's vision includes the nations, then why
are Judah's leaders rejecting their offers to participate in the work?
Zerubbabel's exclusion of foreigners results in immediate antagonism
that plagues the project from beginning to end.

Another sticky issue is the fact that many people of Judah—even
leaders—have married foreign wives. Some of the leaders report to
Ezra, "The people of Israel, including the priests and the Levites, have
not kept themselves separate from the neighboring peoples with
their detestable practices," and by intermarrying they have "mingled
the holy race with the peoples around them" (Eza 9:1-2). Ezra is
devastated, lamenting deeply this unfaithfulness. A member of the

community suggests a solution: "Now let us make a covenant before our God to send away all these women and their children" (Ezra 10:3).

We have no evidence that this idea comes from God or from biblical law, or that a prophetic oracle confirms it as the right approach.[1] The mass divorce this man proposes is simply his own suggestion. All the men agree, so they begin to process cases family by family. When all is said and done, 111 men send their foreign wives packing with all their children.

Later, when the wall is complete, the people gather for a major celebration. Someone reads the Torah aloud, and together they discover a neglected command: "No Ammonite or Moabite should ever be admitted into the assembly of God, because they had not met the Israelites with food and water but had hired Balaam to call a curse down on them" (Nehemiah 13:1-2).

The prohibition comes from Deuteronomy 23, a chapter concerned to define who's in and who's out (Deuteronomy 23:3). The instruction is based on a frustrating episode when the people of Ammon and Moab would not allow the Israelites to peacefully pass through their land on their way to Canaan. Moses had intentionally handed down the memory of this lack of hospitality so that future generations would respond accordingly.

However, the people of Judah both overread and underread this command. For one, they miss its expiration date ("even in the tenth generation"), which has long since passed (Deuteronomy 23:3). Second, rather than excluding only Ammonites and Moabites, "they excluded from Israel *all* who were of foreign descent" (Nehemiah 13:3, emphasis added). They do this even though Deuteronomy 23 explicitly states that after three generations they are welcome to include Egyptians and Edomites, and that escaped slaves are always welcome (Deuteronomy 23:7-8, 15-16). In other words, Deuteronomy 23 is far less stringent about excluding foreigners than the interpretation put forward by the Judeans in Nehemiah's day. If Rahab or Ruth had lived in Judea after the exile, Ezra and Nehemiah would have sent them away because they were foreigners, in spite of their devotion to Yahweh.

We have already considered Jeremiah's letter to the Babylonian exiles encouraging them to marry and put down roots. It presents another possible critique of the Judean policy of exclusion. Jeremiah does not indicate that the Judean exiles are supposed to marry only other Judeans. "Find wives for your sons and give your daughters in marriage" is open-ended (Jeremiah 29:6).

It's also worth considering the words of a contemporary prophet named Malachi. The books of Ezra and Nehemiah do not mention him, but Malachi also addressed the postexilic community, drawing attention to Judah's unfaithfulness: "Judah has desecrated the sanctuary the LORD loves by marrying women who worship a foreign god" (Malachi 2:11). According to Malachi, they should expel the *man* from the community for his unfaithfulness, presumably with his family, since Malachi also insists that each one should be faithful to his marriage covenant (Malachi 2:12-15). Malachi conveys this prophetic oracle: "'The man who hates and divorces his wife,' says the LORD, the God of Israel, 'does violence to the one he should protect,' says the LORD Almighty" (Malachi 2:16).

Was divorce the right answer to the problem of intermarriage? Not according to God's word through the prophet Malachi. Community leaders were wrong to punish the women and their children when it was the men who sinned by marrying them in the first place (if indeed it *was* a sin). Two wrongs do not make a right.

Malachi offers a canonical perspective on the policies of Ezra and Nehemiah. Reading these books together exposes the lack of divine directive for Ezra and Nehemiah. We have no evidence that either sought the Lord for guidance on this specific issue. We don't have an explicit condemnation of their behavior from the narrator. His disapproval is more subtle, similar to the brutal narratives at the end of Judges. The wider testimony of the canon demonstrates the inadequacy of their approach.

CAN WE CRITIQUE THE BIBLE?

If we take seriously Paul's words to Timothy about the Scriptures (which in his day would have only included what we call the Old Testament), then all of it is "God-breathed" and "useful for teaching, rebuking, correcting and training in righteousness" (2 Timothy 3:16). According to the author of Hebrews, "The word of God is alive and active . . . sharper than any double-edged sword" (Hebrews 4:12).

As someone who believes in the inspiration and authority of Scripture, I am not free to discard the parts I don't like. However, we can all agree that not everything the Bible describes is meant for us to imitate. Description is not prescription. Sarah should not have mistreated Hagar. Samson should not have lusted after Philistine women. King Saul should not have spared plunder from his battle with the Amalekites. King David should not have summoned the wife of Uriah to his royal bedroom. Jonah should not have boarded a ship to flee God's commission. Ananias and Sapphira should not have lied about the price of their property.

These are rather obvious conclusions. Others are more complex. Should Abraham have interceded for Isaac rather than offering him on the altar?[a] Was Joseph's method of famine relief in Egypt good or exploitative? Is Elihu's perspective flawed or exemplary in the book of Job? Is the voice of Qohelet in Ecclesiastes a reliable guide to life, or does the narrator intend for us to regard him as a fool? Did the early church leaders make the right decision when they chose a replacement for Judas by casting lots? Was it right for Paul and Barnabas to separate?

The question of how to regard Ezra and Nehemiah is complicated because these books bear their names, which leads to the assumption that they are the authors. Since biblical authors are carried along by the Holy Spirit, doesn't that mean we have to trust them? Yes, we can trust the authors, but we cannot assume that the name of the book indicates authorship. Although these books include first-person ("I") testimony of Ezra and Nehemiah, they also include many stories about them in third person ("he"). That suggests another author compiled the testimonies of Ezra and Nehemiah as part of his own project.

A key to answering this question is to consider the overall shape and literary design of these books as explained in the Bible Project video on Ezra-Nehemiah. Each section of these books ends with an anticlimax—an unpleasant or unsuccessful result of their well-meaning reforms. The last scene depicts Nehemiah yelling at people and pulling out their hair, which hardly seems like exemplary behavior. Both books seem to present the stories of Ezra and Nehemiah as well-intended but unsatisfactory. The narrator is not heavy-handed about it, but perhaps we are supposed to draw our own conclusions about the fruitlessness of their approach.

In other words, I don't disagree with the perspective of the *books* called Ezra and Nehemiah. Rather, I disagree with the *behavior* of the men named Ezra and Nehemiah. Their attempts to follow Torah are skewed because they read it selectively.

LOOK OUT FOR NUMBER ONE

Haggai prophesies after Judah's return from exile. He confronts the community for having their priorities all mixed up. Their logic is that they will work on rebuilding the temple *after* their own houses are in good shape. The magic moment when their affairs are in order and they can turn to Yahweh's work never seems to come.

What they haven't realized is that Yahweh actively frustrates their efforts so that they will revisit their priorities. "'You expected much, but see, it turned out to be little. What you brought home, I blew away. Why?' declares the LORD Almighty. 'Because of my house, which remains a ruin, while each of you is busy with your own house'" (Haggai 1:9).

The people of Judah have things backward. They will never experience God's blessing as long as they undervalue God's presence. They think they are responsible to build wealth for themselves, but God's blessings are available only when they prioritize worship. Without a temple to deal with their ritual and moral defilement, they cannot experience that blessing.

Haggai reassures the people that as soon as they prioritize the presence of God by rebuilding the temple, God will supply abundantly, grant them peace, and bless them. I wonder how many of us need this message. How many of us keep putting off kingdom priorities until we achieve some ideal standard of living or even a sense of being on top of things? What are we missing when we do?

When I was a new mom, my husband, Daniel, took a position as an assistant to the elders at Calvary Mennonite Church near Canby, Oregon. He coordinated the worship team for our Sunday services and attended elders' meetings to take notes and coordinate implementation of the decisions they made. I kept house and looked after our newborn. As part of Daniel's salary, we lived rent-free in the parsonage, a house next door to the church.

> How many of us keep putting off kingdom priorities until we achieve some ideal standard of living or even a sense of being on top of things? What are we missing when we do?

One highlight of the week for me was walking next door each Wednesday morning for the Women's Missionary Society meetings.

These women had been meeting for decades to sew quilts to be auctioned off to raise funds for missions. Usually, we had two quilts going at once—a simple block pattern tufted with yarn or embroidery thread, and a more elaborate pieced quilt with impressive hand-quilted patterns. The fancy quilt was stretched across a large frame that could accommodate eight or more women quilting at a time around its edges. As each end of the quilt was completed, we would roll it tightly around the outer frame and clamp it again to the side rails so that we could reach more areas that needed quilting. At this weekly meeting, I would lay our baby on a blanket on the floor nearby with some toys. Then I would choose a needle and start stitching. While we sewed, we would share the latest news. Vacations, family milestones, gardening tips, things we saw on the news or read in the papers, books we were reading. After a couple of hours of sewing, we'd stop for lunch.

As the months ticked away, my baby was soon crawling and eventually toddling around the room. She walked early, at just nine months old, so she was still short enough to fit under the quilt frame. We'd see the little bump of her head roaming around under the quilt.

These women were wise enough not to try to tell me how to raise her, even when I asked their advice. I'd puzzle over some current struggle, such as how to get her to stop sucking her fingers or establish a better sleep schedule. They'd shrug and say, "That was so long ago. Everything is different now, and I don't even remember!" I was in my early twenties at the time. The next youngest woman in the room after me was almost forty years my senior, and she was a good bit younger than the next. The oldest was over one hundred. Our group wasn't career driven, but these women were faithful. Steady. Serving week after week and sending stacks of quilts every year to be auctioned off for missions. For a while it bothered me that they didn't have more advice to offer. Now that my own children are reaching adulthood, I understand their hesitancy. The older I get, the less parenting advice I have to offer.

What the women modeled for me more than anything else was the power of consistent service. They showed up week after week to donate their time for a cause that mattered to them. These women funded the international relief and development work of the Mennonite Central Committee by donating their Wednesday mornings. The group had been meeting consistently since the church was founded in 1944.

When our time came to go overseas as missionaries, the women supplied a quilt for our auction and baked pies to sell. They also wrote a check every month to support us, taken from donations from their members. And they prayed. Their shared commitment to this work bonded them to each other, cultivating friendship that carried them through the decades.

Think about what I would have missed in friendship and support if I'd hung out only with my peers. And think what their work made possible in God's global mission. They could have chosen to stay at home and scrub their own kitchens or sew quilts for their own grandchildren or watch soap operas. Instead, they invested four or five hours a week to generate income for mission projects they would never see with their own eyes.

I think Haggai would have been a big fan of the Women's Missionary Society. A community that works together for the sake of kingdom priorities is a place where God's Spirit moves.

A FEW GOOD MEN

It turns out that not every Jewish family cultivated these kinds of priorities. Once the temple was rebuilt, even the priests were lazy about sacrifices, offering God diseased rather than unblemished animals (Malachi 1:6-14). The people lived openly in sin while bringing their offerings, expecting God to overlook their unfaithfulness. And they skimped on the tithe required by the law (Malachi 3:8-12).

Worst of all, they badmouthed the whole idea of serving God: "What do we gain by carrying out his requirements and going about like mourners before the Lord Almighty? But now we call the arrogant blessed. Certainly, evildoers prosper, and even when they put God to the test, they get away with it" (Malachi 3:14-15). For many of the people of Judah, following Yahweh was not worth the effort. They were convinced that they were just as well off doing evil.

However, not everyone fit this profile. A few people were dismayed by the apostasy of their generation. They rallied together and renewed their commitment to covenant faithfulness. Yahweh took notice and said something remarkable about this righteous remnant: "'On the day when I act,' says the Lord Almighty, 'they will be my treasured possession [*segullah*]. I will spare them, just as a father has compassion and spares his son who serves him. And you will again see the distinction between the righteous and the wicked, between those who serve God and those who do not'" (Malachi 3:17-18).

Segullah ("treasured possession") is my favorite Hebrew word. It's a technical term used in ancient treaties to indicate a favored treaty partner who bears special responsibilities. God first uses it of Israel in Exodus 19:5-6, when he announces Israel's covenant status.

Malachi echoes that moment here, but with a fascinating twist. For the first time in the Hebrew Bible, *segullah* refers to a subgroup rather than the entire nation. These men and women who cling faithfully to the worship of Yahweh and who align with God's kingdom priorities—*they alone* will be God's treasured possession.

Special covenant status will not apply to every person of Jewish descent but only to those who live in submission to God's reign and honor him as holy. This is downright revolutionary. It anticipates

Paul's teaching in Romans 9:6, "Not all who are descended from Israel are Israel." It also forms the basis for Peter's declaration in 1 Peter 2:9 that the church in Asia Minor, made up of Jewish *and* Gentile followers of Jesus, is "God's special possession." Redefining covenant membership apart from natural citizenship is a game changer. In Malachi's vision, a remnant of the people of Israel formed a new family characterized by faithfulness to God.

When we lived overseas as missionaries, we became part of a community of believers that acted like an extended family. We spent holidays, celebrated birthdays, and took vacations together. We prayed together. That feeling of family started even before we arrived, when our new teammates, Phil and Julie, paid for our ministry training course and took the time to visit our parents and siblings in the States to get to know them. We shared meals together as we prepared to serve together.

Our children called them "Grandpa Phil and Grandma Julie." When we returned to the United States, Phil and Julie soon followed, retiring just a mile from where we lived. We were across the country from our biological families, serving in our mission headquarters, so our surrogate family connection continued. When we moved west and Phil and Julie moved to our mission's retirement village in Florida, our connection continued across the miles. They visited us in Oregon, and we visited them in Florida.

Back in Oregon near our biological family, another couple from our mission moved just a mile away. Willy and Angela served as regional directors for recruitment and training. They became like family to us as well, with an added twist. Since we lived near our biological family, they had an opportunity to get to know one another. Willy and Angela became a fixture whenever we gathered at our home for Thanksgiving, Christmas, or Easter.

Being part of the faith community results in new family ties with those who are not biologically related. That positive development of family ties sometimes results in distancing from our biological family when values do not align. Jesus redefined family in radical ways:

For I have come to turn

"a man against his father,
    a daughter against her mother,
a daughter-in-law against her mother-in-law—
    a man's enemies will be the members of his
        own household."

Anyone who loves their father or mother more than me is not worthy of me; anyone who loves their son or daughter more than me is not worthy of me. Whoever does not take up their cross and follow me is not worthy of me. Whoever finds their life will lose it, and whoever loses their life for my sake will find it. (Matthew 10:35-39)

This is not a license to be a jerk to our family members. Rather, it reckons with the reality that following Jesus may put us at odds with our blood family. We are to prioritize faithfulness to God rather than bend our beliefs or behavior to accommodate those who are not following Jesus. According to the Bible, our truest family is the family of fellow believers. While the Bible itself does not give examples of this costly decision to follow Jesus that results in family rejection, church history is full of examples, especially in the Muslim world. Those who recognize Jesus as king are often disowned by their families.

> According to the Bible, our truest family is the family of fellow believers.

THIS IS US

Isaiah joins Malachi to offer a surprising guest list to the covenant community. After the exile, as we've seen, nationalist ideals run high among those committed to rebuilding the temple. Isaiah 56–66 addresses the postexilic context with a grand vision that includes some unexpected developments. It's interesting to imagine how Ezra and Nehemiah might have felt about it.

The people of Israel are upset because their prayers are not being answered (Isaiah 58:3-5). Yahweh tells them their community must be characterized by action for the victims of injustice, the hungry, the poor, and the naked. Isaiah calls the needy "your own flesh and blood" (Isaiah 58:7). If we want to experience the healing presence of Yahweh in our communities, then we must adjust our thinking about those in need. Until we recognize that they belong to us and we belong to them, we will never experience the flourishing God intends for us.

According to Isaiah, foreigners "bound to Yahweh" are to be included (Isaiah 56:3), and foreigners who serve Yahweh will be welcome to bring sacrifices to the temple and keep his covenant (Isaiah 56:6). The prophet's vision is not nationalistic; he delivers God's declaration: "'My house will be called a house of prayer for all nations.' The Sovereign LORD declares—he who gathers the exiles of Israel: 'I will gather still others to them besides those already gathered'" (Isaiah 56:8). The "still others" evidently includes non-Israelites. God is building a multiethnic family. In a world sharply divided between "us" and "them," God is redrawing the line.

Yahweh will also give eunuchs "a memorial and a name better than sons and daughters" (Isaiah 56:5). This is remarkable. A eunuch is a man unable to father children either because of a birth defect or (more commonly) a surgical procedure required for certain government jobs, such as overseeing the king's harem. In the ancient world, a eunuch gave up his own future for the sake of the king. Without children of his own, his life was a mere breath—here today and gone tomorrow. Children were the measure of longevity. Ancient people were more concerned about the continuation of their family line than they were about the length of their own life. But the prophet says that God will give eunuchs "an everlasting name that will endure forever"—precisely what they lack (Isaiah 56:5).

Isaiah closes with a vision of God sending messengers to the most far-flung nations—Spain, North Africa, Greece, and distant islands—to proclaim God's glory. As a result, "'They will bring all your people, from all the nations, to my holy mountain in Jerusalem as an offering to the LORD. . . . And I will select some of them also to be priests and Levites,' says the LORD" (Isaiah 66:20-21). The presence of people from other nations will not be a threat but a blessing. They will be invited to participate at a level that even most Israelites have not experienced—serving as priests in the temple. "Your people," the prophet calls them. Earlier he describes these nations as family: "Your sons come from afar, and your daughters are carried on the hip" (Isaiah 60:4).

> The presence of people from other nations will not be a threat but a blessing.

Your people.

Your sons.

Your daughters.

The poor. The foreigner. The eunuch.

This is us.

Psalm 87 also celebrates the multiethnic family of faith. It speaks of Jerusalem as God's treasured place in which the names of Egyptians, Babylonians, Philistines, Phoenicians, and Africans will be recorded as true believers and native-born citizens. If we are not of Jewish descent, then we are the fulfillment of these prophetic visions.

As followers of Jesus, we have joined the covenant family as a "king-dom of priests" (Exodus 19:6; see 1 Peter 2:9). Called to be part of this faith community, we have become part of the worldwide family of God. That makes you my mother, father, sister, brother, daughter, or son in the faith.

Have you ever traveled internationally and unexpectedly met another Christian? My friend Jennifer traveled to France for research.[2] One of the library aides noticed she kept asking to see old French Bibles. The woman whispered to her in French, "Are you a Christian?"

"Yes!" my friend answered. "How did you know?" The aide explained that no one cared about these old Bibles. The two women embraced like old friends, having found each other in a sea of people who did not share their allegiance to the Jewish Messiah.

The boundaries of this family keep growing wider. They encompass anyone and everyone who surrenders to Yahweh's kingship expressed in Jesus the Messiah. This is one reason why a sermon on YouTube is a poor substitute for our full, embodied participation in the life of the church. Something happens when we gather and join hands and make eye contact that cannot happen solo. We begin to belong to one another. We become God's family.

This is us.

BONUS MATERIAL (CHRONICLES)

About a hundred years after the book of Kings was written, someone decided it was time to retell the story. The Chronicler did not start from scratch. He (or they, if it was a group effort) began with core stories taken from Samuel and Kings, adding new material along the way so that the finished product included half old stories and half new stories.

I was a teaching assistant in college for one of my professors, who asked me to carefully read Chronicles and highlight anything that did not come directly from Samuel and Kings. It was a wonderful exercise. What became very clear was that the bonus material revolves around two major themes: David and the temple. While the book of Kings focuses primarily on the Northern Kingdom of Israel until they are dragged into exile, Chronicles focuses almost exclusively on the Southern Kingdom of Judah, where David's descendants reign.

Unlike 2 Samuel, the stories about David in Chronicles are thoroughly positive. We don't read about his massive failure when he took the wife of Uriah. We hear nothing of his inability to keep his adult sons in line. Does the Chronicler hope we will forget what we know about him? Not likely. The Chronicler is not trying to trick us into thinking David is perfect. But those stories would be a distraction from the point the Chronicler is trying to make. His goal is to offer positive stories as examples to follow.

In Chronicles, we hear for the first time about David's preparations for building the temple. His son Solomon is the one who eventually builds it, but David gathers many of the supplies. Although both Kings and Chronicles recount the temple dedication, the account in Chronicles provides more detail. Chronicles also highlights temple repairs under five different kings of Judah: Asa, Joash, Jotham, Hezekiah, and Josiah.

Alongside his focus on the temple, the Chronicler highlights the importance of heart attitudes in worship, and he includes many long prayers that do not appear in Samuel and Kings. What is the point of all this bonus material?

One hundred years after going into exile, the Judeans have returned to the land of Canaan. Their primary task is to rebuild the temple, which makes the stories about the historic temple of utmost importance. By zeroing in on the preparation, building, dedication, and repair of the temple, the Chronicler hopes to cultivate interest in corporate worship and provide an example to follow. This project would be the defining achievement of that generation. They could not afford to miss the mark.

The Chronicler understands our human need to be part of something larger than ourselves—to participate in work that truly matters. What could be more important than reestablishing sacred space amid the community?

Chronicles features only positive stories about David, with one exception. The story of David's census in 1 Chronicles 21 is the only story from 1–2 Samuel critical of David that the Chronicler chooses to include. This unflattering story of David's failure to trust God and the consequences he endures is necessary to the larger purposes of the book.

To understand why, we must pay close attention to the consequences of David's actions. David calls for a military census against the advice of his commander. The exercise is simply a flex of David's power and a failure to trust God's protection. After the numbers are in, David realizes immediately that he has sinned, and he prays for forgiveness.

God allows David to choose his own consequence from three options: "three years of famine, three months of being swept away before your enemies . . . or three days of the sword of the LORD—days of plague in the land, with the angel of the LORD ravaging every part of Israel" (1 Chronicles 21:12). David chooses the last option, putting himself and his nation in God's hands.

The plague is indeed devastating, with many unfortunate deaths due to David's folly. However, in the midst of judgment, Yahweh has compassion on the nation and stops his angel from further destruction. The narrator tells us, "The angel of the LORD was then standing at the threshing floor of Araunah the Jebusite" (1 Chronicles 21:15).

This location is of paramount importance to the overall plot of the book. A threshing floor was the place where people processed their grain harvests by dragging heavy equipment over stalks of wheat to separate the grain from the straw and chaff. Whenever possible, they carried out this work on a hilltop so that the wind could easily carry away the chaff, leaving the nutrient-rich grain behind.

David purchases this prime hilltop real estate from the Jebusite and builds an altar there to offer burnt offerings and fellowship offerings to God. David has already repented. These offerings are his way of expressing gratitude and restoring fellowship with Yahweh. Remarkably, "The LORD answered him with fire from heaven on the altar of burnt offering" (1 Chronicles 21:26). This dramatic response mirrors the one that took place when the tabernacle was built; fire fell on the altar then too (Leviticus 9:24). David logically concludes that this is the perfect place to build the temple. He says, "The house of the LORD God is to be here, and also the altar of burnt offering for Israel" (1 Chronicles 22:1).

Why tell this unflattering story about David in a book that offers an otherwise unflaggingly positive picture of him? The census debacle is essential because it secures the location of the temple—the other key theme of the book of Chronicles. In this very place, God shows mercy and provides dramatic evidence of his presence and blessing.

The placement of Chronicles in the biblical canon affects how we hear it. In our English Bibles, the books of Chronicles appear immediately after Samuel and Kings and before Ezra and Nehemiah. This makes the book feel redundant if we're reading the Bible straight through. Immediately after reading the stories for the first time, we read many of them again. We may wonder why.

In the three-part Hebrew Bible, the books are arranged differently. Samuel and Kings are part of the second major section, the "Former Prophets," while Chronicles is part of the last section, the "Writings." In fact, Chronicles is the last book in the Hebrew Bible. Rather than repeating what has just been said (as it seems to do in our English Bibles), Chronicles revisits it from a much later perspective.

This is why 2 Chronicles ends with an invitation, penned by Cyrus king of Persia. Here is my own translation of the Hebrew, to help capture the distinctive word order of his statement: "Thus says Cyrus, King of Persia, 'Yahweh the God of heaven has given to me all the kingdoms of the earth. He himself has appointed me to build him a house in Jerusalem, which is in Judah. Whoever among you from all his people has Yahweh his God with him, let him go up'" (2 Chronicles 36:23). The book ends with a hanging invitation to "go up." Go up and do what? The implication is obvious, after reading Chronicles. Those who desire to experience the presence of God ought to go up and do what so many of the kings of Judah have done: to build or restore the temple. For Jewish readers, the entire Hebrew Bible closes with this dangling invitation to participate in building a community centered on the very presence of God.

Ironically, in the Hebrew Bible, the books of Ezra and Nehemiah, with their fuller account of the decree of Cyrus along with its fulfillment, come *before* Chronicles. Perhaps the message is that the rebuilding work that had already happened was somehow unfinished. When Solomon built the temple, the fire and glory of God's presence descended on it, just as it had at Sinai (2 Chronicles 7:1). However, after the exile, no glory enveloped the rebuilt temple. Without a visitation of the presence of God, more work remained. The people must engage in the work of prayer and repentance so that they are fit to have God's presence among them. As long as we see others as the enemy rather than as potential family members, we have not become the community God desires.

Why would it be any different for us? Thousands of years later, we are still at our best when we faithfully gather in multiethnic

communities to wait for the presence of God and to carry out the
work he gave us to do.

KEY IDEAS

- The books of Ezra and Nehemiah depict the failed attempts of
  those who returned from exile to reestablish a community that
  honored God. The leaders exhibit a selective reading of the Torah
  and lack of consideration for the words of the prophets.

- A community that works together for the sake of kingdom
  priorities is a place where God's Spirit moves.

- The boundaries of God's multiethnic family keep expanding
  to include anyone who surrenders to his kingship.

- The Hebrew Bible closes with an invitation to participate in
  building a community centered on the very presence of God.

DIGGING DEEPER

Aaron Chalmers. *Interpreting the Prophets: Reading, Understanding and Preaching from the Worlds of the Prophets*. IVP
Academic, 2015.

David M. Howard. *An Introduction to the Old Testament Historical
Books*. Moody, 1993.

Related videos from BibleProject: "Ezra-Nehemiah," "1 &
2 Chronicles," and "Holy Spirit."

8

FAMILY REUNION

THICKER THAN BLOOD

Matthew introduces us to Jesus not as a standout talent or a successful public figure who has made something of himself but as one who takes his place in an enormous family tree. He is the most recent son in a long line of sons born into the family of Abraham. Surveying key moments of Jesus' Old Testament background first will highlight key features of his ministry we might otherwise miss.

One thing to notice is that five women appear in Matthew's genealogy of Jesus—an unusual addition. Several factors make their presence interesting. The women were not Israelites (in the case of Tamar, Rahab, Ruth, and probably the wife of Uriah, since he was a Hittite) and the circumstances by which they conceived were unusual (in the cases of Tamar, Ruth, Mary, and the wife of Uriah). Aside from the patriarchs (Abraham, Isaac, and Jacob), we know next to nothing about any of the wives of other men on this list. These women appear here because their stories are important to the plot. Each of them demonstrated loyalty to the God of Israel and to the survival of his people. Without them, we don't have Christmas.

Another feature of this genealogy often escapes notice. Matthew introduces these four women not as wives but as mothers. Rahab is not called the wife of Salmon but the mother of Boaz. Ruth is not presented as the wife of Boaz but as the mother of Obed. Why does this detail matter?

Matthew presents Jesus not just as an Israelite but as "the Messiah, the son of David, the son of Abraham" (Matthew 1:1). For Jesus to be a son of David indicates his rightful place in the line of the kings of Judah. The records of the monarchy in Samuel, Kings, and Chronicles introduce each king along with his mother, not his wife. The spouses of a monarch were not considered queens of Israel and Judah. (This would have caused a great deal of confusion anyway, since they all had multiple wives.) Instead, the kingdoms of Israel and Judah had queen mothers. The most powerful woman in the kingdom was the mother of the king. She would have had a throne beside her son and wielded significant influence.

To introduce Jesus alongside the name of his mother is the traditional way to introduce him as Judah's rightful *king*. Matthew gives us many clues in Matthew 1 that he sees Jesus as a king in the line of David and as the culmination of Israel's story. By presenting the genealogy in three parts with fourteen generations each (noted explicitly in Matthew 1:17), Matthew neatly divides Israel's history into eras: the covenant with Abraham, the kingship of David, and the age of the exile. The coming of Jesus signals the end of the exile and the beginning of a new era.

Matthew's focus on Jesus as a member of Abraham's family is bolstered by Luke's genealogy, which traces the line of Jesus all the way back to Adam, the father of humanity. Matthew's inclusion of Gentile women and Luke's extension past Abraham confirm that Gentiles have a place in God's family. According to Luke, Adam is the "son of God" (Luke 3:38; see Genesis 5:1-3).

However, Jesus is not just any human. He takes his place in the very particular family of Abraham, for whom God's promises were coming true with Jesus' arrival. Matthew's account of Jesus' birth and early ministry highlights episodes that mirror those of the nation of Israel.

The Israelites sojourn in Egypt; so does Jesus as a child.

The Israelites spend forty years being tested in the desert; Jesus spends forty days undergoing similar tests in the wilderness.

Israel crosses the Jordan River and enters the Promised Land; John baptizes Jesus in the Jordan before he begins his ministry.

Israel consists of twelve tribes; Jesus calls twelve disciples, reconstituting the nation around himself.

Isaiah had identified Israel as God's chosen servant sent to do his work, but Isaiah also spoke of an individual servant who would restore Israel to God. Matthew presents Jesus as that servant (Matthew 12:15-21). Daniel's "son of man" was an individual who represented the people of God; Jesus fulfills this representative role.

Given his context in a family-oriented culture, Jesus expresses his most shocking words when his family members come to speak with him. Jesus asks, "'Who is my mother, and who are my brothers?' Pointing to his disciples, he said, 'Here are my mother and my brothers. For whoever does the will of my Father in heaven is my brother and sister and mother'" (Matthew 12:48-50). Jesus does not discard his biological family. They too are invited to "hear God's word and put it into practice" (Luke 8:21). But Jesus redefines family around himself. Membership in his family is not by marriage or by genealogical descent but by allegiance to Jesus as King. He tells the people, "everyone who has left houses or brothers or sisters or father or mother or wife or children or fields for my sake will receive a hundred times as much and will inherit eternal life" (Matthew 19:29).

These words are radical in the modern world, and they were unthinkable in Jesus' day. Family loyalties ran higher than anything else. Jesus dismantles those allegiances and rebuilds them around kingdom purposes. His followers are to be as loyal to one another as they have been raised to be in their biological families.

Westerners often think of marriages as the building blocks of society. However, in the first century, sibling relationships were primary. A wife was more likely to feel a close emotional bond with her brother than her husband, even long after getting married.[1] Knowing this helps us understand the significance of sibling language in the New Testament. When Jesus speaks of his followers as "brothers and sisters," he's tapping into the deepest and most loyal bond anyone in the Mediterranean world experienced. If you become my brother, it means I will drop anything to help you.

> When Jesus speaks of his followers as "brothers and sisters," he's tapping into the deepest and most loyal bond anyone in the Mediterranean world experienced.

Depending on your culture and family of origin, the sibling metaphor may not resonate with you. While we need not abandon our cultural ideas about family to try to recreate a first-century scenario, we should hear what Jesus is saying about the church with his cultural values in mind. If we are all siblings, then Jesus expects us to prioritize one another's needs.

Sometimes people talk as though single adults are not yet full-fledged human beings, or as though their lives are on hold until they find "the one." However, the Christian faith holds no expectation that believers marry. In fact, Jesus and Paul were both single. New Testament scholar David Bennett notes that biblically speaking, "Marriage is not ultimate or even the greatest form of intimacy that can be experienced, as is often wrongly communicated by the church and our society at large. Rather the love of friendship is the greatest of the loves."[2]

Because sibling relationships are primary in the faith community, the doors are wide open for singles, marrieds, and people of all ages. One woman I know intentionally sits with single friends in church rather than with her husband to practically demonstrate to herself and others that the family of faith ought to be our priority.[3] Her husband does the same. That is a bold idea. As believers we don't just bring our families to church. We come to church because it is our family.

Those of us from individualistic contexts find it challenging to think of ourselves as beholden to anyone, kin or not. For us, Jesus' call to belong to one another is costly, requiring us to radically rethink our priorities. For those from cultural contexts in which family loyalties are paramount, Jesus' call to become family with other believers is equally costly. In some cultural contexts, to belong to other believers can be seen as a betrayal of blood relatives.

They say blood is thicker than water, but Jesus introduces a bond even thicker than blood—the family of faith. After spending all night in prayer on a mountain, Jesus comes down and chooses twelve men to follow him, in effect replaying the Sinai event and reconstituting the nation around himself (Luke 6:12-16). Female disciples travel with him as well (Luke 8:1-3).

Although Jesus' primary focus is to reconcile the estranged members of God's covenant family, he also challenges the ethnocentrism of his disciples by ministering in Tyre and Sidon, which hints at God's wider purposes for non-Jewish people (Luke 6:17). Jesus commends the faith of a Roman centurion, the ultimate symbol of the empire hated by the Jews (Matthew 8:5-13). He tells his disciples, "Many will come from the east and the west, and will take their places at the feast with Abraham, Isaac and Jacob in the kingdom of heaven.

But the subjects of the kingdom will be thrown outside, into the darkness, where there will be weeping and gnashing of teeth" (Matthew 8:11-12). Gentiles will be welcome at God's table, and some insiders will be sent away.

This should give us pause as we think about the church today. Who's "in" who has not surrendered to Jesus' kingship? Who's "out" whom Jesus would invite to join us? What would happen if we recognized that the church is not a social club, but a faith family oriented around the rule of King Jesus?

CHILDREN AMONG THE DISCIPLES

The Christian faith is always one generation away from extinction. Think of Judges 2:10: "After that whole generation had been gathered to their ancestors, another generation grew up who knew neither the LORD nor what he had done for Israel." If we fail to pass on the faith, or the next generation refuses to embrace it, Christianity fades into obscurity, and our church buildings stand empty, like so many of Europe's cathedrals. Before Moses died, he passed along a vision of family discipleship in which parents nurtured their children in the faith day in and day out. He charged them, "These commandments that I give you today are to be on your hearts. Impress them on your children. Talk about them when you sit at home and when you walk along the road, when you lie down and when you get up" (Deuteronomy 6:6-7). Children were invited participants at Israel's sacrifices and feasts, which was a crucial part of their formation as covenant members (Deuteronomy 12:12; 16:18).

Jesus lived out this value by spending time with children, welcoming them as disciples. What would it look like if we took seriously the idea that children also follow Jesus—that they are not just *future* disciples but disciples right now? We can learn so much from children if we take the time to be with them.

Robbie Castleman points out that we make great efforts to be on time for athletic games or concerts because we don't want to miss the kickoff or the opening notes. We train our children to pursue excellence in musical ability, in sports, and in academics. Why don't we train them in worship? Most will never be professional athletes or musicians, but we'll all be professional worshipers in the new creation.[a]

At twelve years old, I developed a weekly program for the children of my parents' small group from church. Rather than simply turn on a movie (although we did that, too, because the meetings lasted for hours), we had Bible lessons, coloring and crafts, and Bible memory.

At fourteen years old, I went on my first of two summer mission trips to Central and South America. Our church commissioned me with their hearty blessing.

At sixteen years old, our pastor appointed me as missions coordinator for our church. I gave monthly updates during the Sunday service about our church's missionaries around the world.

At eighteen years old, the same pastor invited me to teach a summer class for adults, based on what I had learned in my first year at Bible college. He required all the elders and ministry leaders of the church to attend my class.

Not every teenager has the sense of calling to ministry that I did or the courage to follow through. But many more of them do than we realize. When I reflect now on the ways that the adults in my life took me seriously as a fellow disciple, I wonder whether I've done the same for the children and youth I've encountered since then. Do I see them as fellow followers of Jesus? Am I willing to learn from children?

My friend Kaitlyn Schiess has a delightful podcast called *Curiously, Kaitlyn*, where kids ask questions about God and the Bible. She takes these questions seriously by bringing on scholars to answer them. She is convinced that we can learn much from children.

Recently, we visited a church in Chicago for the first time. I was delighted to find this notice on their website: "Children are essential participants in the life of our church. They are not the future of the church, they are the church today!"[b] A church we visited in Texas has a quiet play area to the side of the sanctuary where children can listen to the message while their little hands are busy.

According to the prophet Joel, a key marker of covenant renewal and the outpouring of the Spirit is that "your sons and daughters will prophesy" (Joel 2:28). Young and old will experience the empowering of the Spirit to participate in God's mission. Sometimes churches today treat children as though they simply need to be entertained while mom and dad engage in real worship. On the contrary, they are fellow disciples!

I vividly remember a Good Friday service we attended with our children. Easton was almost four years old. The somber music and darkened sanctuary set the tone for the devastating news: Jesus had been crucified. Easton wept. He was not throwing a fit because he wanted a snack or because he was bored. Easton was truly devastated to learn that his Savior had been killed. People glared at us as if to say we should remove our son from the service. But it didn't seem right to leave. Easton had entered the true spirit of the service as much as any adult in that room. He was leading us in worship.

AN UNLIKELY ENGAGEMENT

Following King Jesus is an adventure because Jesus regularly acts in surprising ways. We can learn about what sort of community he's trying to build by watching him closely. In John 3, people question John the Baptist, assuming that Jesus is an emerging rival to his ministry. After all, Jesus is also baptizing people, drawing significant crowds, including some who used to follow John. To the Jewish leaders, that smacks of competition. John sees things differently.

Using the metaphor of a wedding, John the Baptist explains that he is the *friend* of the groom, not the groom. God sends John ahead of the Messiah to prepare the way, as a groomsman helps to prepare for the wedding day. The arrival of the groom cannot be construed as competition because the plan from the beginning is to focus on him and his bride.

In John's Gospel, the next event is Jesus' journey through Samaria, where he sits down by a well. Readers familiar with the Old Testament narratives might perk up at this point. In Genesis, when a man arrives at a well, he typically meets a woman, and by the end of the scene they are married. This is not to say that betrothals always happened at wells or that men regularly hung out at wells to find a wife. Obviously, most trips to the well do not result in a wedding. However, Genesis and Exodus set up a narrative pattern in which Isaac, Jacob, and Moses each find a wife in this way.

Jesus, uncharacteristically alone, sits down at a well in the heat of the day in Samaria, the heart of the old Northern Kingdom. A woman comes to draw water, and he engages her in conversation by asking for a drink. Their conversation is unconventional. He is a Jew. She is a Samaritan, descended from those who repopulated the region after the exile of the Northern Kingdom. That probably means she has mixed ancestry—part Jewish and part foreigner. Historically, Jews avoided having anything to do with the Samaritans, whom they suspected of religious compromise and unfaithfulness. However, Jesus is not deterred by this history. He exhibits none of the ethnocentrism she has come to expect.

Their conversation is also unusual because out of extreme piety, Jewish men avoided talking with women who were not family members. When Jesus' disciples return later, they are "surprised to find him talking with a woman" (John 4:27). By asking her for a drink, Jesus violates two social norms—since she is a Samaritan and a woman—treating her as family. Their conversation quickly turns theological, another surprise, as well as personal, discussing her marital status. Then comes the biggest surprise of all. For the first time, Jesus openly admits that he is the long-awaited Messiah.

Why choose this moment to reveal his identity? Jesus has not directly revealed his identity and purpose to anyone up to this point—not even his own disciples. This unnamed woman, whom church tradition calls Photini, runs back to her village without her water jar to call everyone to come meet Jesus. They come in response to her testimony and believe Jesus' message.

The ultimate proof of their mutual acceptance is their extension of hospitality. Jesus offers living water to Photini. Her village feeds and houses Jesus and his disciples for two days. Jesus' willingness to subvert expectations results in the dismantling of boundaries between the two groups.

For readers wondering whether this scene will end with a wedding, it sort of does. Two families have become one, united around faith in Jesus of Nazareth as the Messiah. The Bible describes Christ's eventual return as a wedding—a groom returning for his bride. And here's the thing: God is not a polygamist. Jesus does not have more than one bride. We are together his bride. If we want union with Christ, we must come together as one. We don't get to pick and choose who can worship alongside us today, and we certainly don't get to pick and choose who will join us in the new creation.

> We don't get to pick and choose who can worship alongside us today, and we certainly don't get to pick and choose who will join us in the new creation.

To join the family of faith is to join a multinational and intergenerational community whose boundaries slice through our prejudice and subvert our expectations. He opens the door for everyone, even Samaritans. Joining this family requires that we surrender worldly values and leave behind false ways of sorting people into categories of who's in and who's out.

WORLD UPSIDE DOWN

The message Jesus' disciples carry to the nations makes waves, challenging the most deeply held convictions and values of the Roman Empire. It is a countercultural movement. We can especially see this in the ministry of the apostle Paul in Acts. When Paul casts a demon out of a young slave woman in Philippi, it lands him in jail (Acts 16). The slave owners accuse Paul of "throwing our city into an uproar by advocating customs unlawful for us Romans to accept or practice" (Acts 16:20). Paul's message is not just countercultural; they deem it "unlawful."

In his book *World Upside Down*, Kavin Rowe argues that Paul's sermon in Athens in Acts 17 is likewise contentious. Rowe points to clues in the narrative that indicate Paul is not just having a friendly philosophical discussion in the Areopagus, but rather the philosophers have "seized" him and forced him to testify before the Council. Their accusations mirror those made against Socrates more than four hundred years earlier—that he had brought "strange" teaching and advocated for "new" and "foreign gods"—the same accusations that had resulted in Socrates's death sentence.[4]

Paul skillfully defends himself against these charges using Athenian literature and concepts, insisting that the God he announces is the Creator and therefore not newly invented. By evoking Greek culture, Paul does not accommodate the Christian faith to pagan philosophy. Rather, his speech shows Athenian philosophy to be inadequate, since it has failed to bring people into a living relationship with the God whose name they do not even know. Paul issues a clear call to reject pagan idolatry, saying, "In the past God

overlooked such ignorance, but now he commands all people every-
where to repent" (Acts 17:30).[5]

The political implications of Paul's religious teaching might be
hard for modern readers to grasp. However, to worship a "new" God
was tantamount to insurrection. As Siu Fung Wu explains, "Caesar,
the Roman emperor, was considered to be a representative of the
gods, and his successful military campaigns were seen as signs of
divine favor. The peace and prosperity of the Empire showed that
the gods were on the side of Caesar, which, in turn, legitimized his
rule."[6] To worship Jesus as Lord instead was to put oneself at odds
with the Roman Empire, refusing to worship the emperor or his
sponsoring deities.

Paul and Jesus never suggest a plan to establish alternate worldly
forms of power. Replacing one leader with a less problematic one
does not ultimately solve the issue of human society that operates on
worldly principles. We are called instead to a countercultural way of
life built on humility, not power. That new way of life is characterized
by love of God and neighbor and most of all by waiting for a transcendent God to break in from the outside to heal our broken world.

To appreciate the radical nature of the fledgling community of
faith in the Roman Empire, we must understand their context. In
the first century, the concept of family honor was paramount. The
family you were born into mostly determined how you would be
received by the wider society. A man's children inherited his honor,
which included positive public regard as well as an expectation to
benefit others. Resources were freely shared within a household,
while wealthy families became benefactors to the broader society by
leveraging their wealth for the public good and receiving honor
in return.

Paul harnessed this honor system and took it in a startling new
direction by describing the church as a family. Believers who were

not related by blood began sharing resources as if they were members of one household. In the first century, only 10 percent of the population had what could be considered extra income, 25 percent lived just above subsistence level—one crisis away from poverty—and 65 percent lived at or below that level.[7] The wealthiest members of society were expected to benefit the common good by funding public projects. In so doing, they accrued honor. In the church, things were different. Those with means donated directly to church leaders. For example, in Acts 4:32-37, believers sell their property and relinquish the proceeds to the apostles, who distribute it to those in need. By allowing church leaders to redistribute the funds as they saw fit, donors did not receive public honor or recognition as benefactors. Rather, they shared what they had with other believers as if they were family.[8]

If you're familiar with the story of Ananias and Sapphira in Acts 5, this background explains why their behavior is so problematic. They sell land and donate *part* of the money under pretense of great generosity, acting as if it is the full amount. They miss the memo. They are still seeking the honor associated with public benefaction rather than viewing fellow believers as members of their own family. Ananias and Sapphira treat the church as a social network where they can increase their own standing. The Holy Spirit takes their hypocrisy *very* seriously. They both fall dead on the spot.

To join the Christian community is to join a family. Anyone who does so must be prepared to share their resources accordingly.

UNLIKELY COMPANIONS

We were an unlikely pair. Donna stood 4'10" or so at her full height. Wisps of unruly white hair framed her face. She was unmarried and had no children of her own. She earned a small income from caring for two young women with intellectual disabilities who lived with her in a small apartment. Donna had no vehicle and was unable to drive. She was also physically challenged. Having chain-smoked for most of her adult life, her lungs wheezed if she tried to walk places. She relied entirely on busses and rides from friends and other members of the church.

I was fifteen. Once a week, my mom would drop me off at Donna's doorstep. We'd spend an hour or so together, and then Mom would pick me up and bring me home. What brought us together? Donna and I would sit at the tiny square laminate table in her kitchen and hunker down over her prayer notebook, reading missionary letters and praying over them together. Donna had the biggest heart for missions of anyone I knew. She scrimped and saved however she could so that she could support as many missionaries as possible.

At the time, I was preparing to go on my second short-term mission trip. Often, at the end of our time praying together for missionaries she would get out her checkbook and write me a check for $15. She wanted to participate in sharing the gospel in places she couldn't go herself. It's hard to think of what else might pull together a fifteen-year-old in the flurry of her high school years with a semi-retired, disabled elderly woman. But there we were, brought together by a common purpose. We were family. We were the church.

When Donna died, our family became certified so that we could be a host family for one of the developmentally disabled women who had lived with her. Jeanne had stayed temporarily with Donna, and we fell in love with her. She moved in with us during my senior year of high school for about a year.

This sort of thing happens all the time in the church—or at least it can if we watch for it and make space. These days, older folks and younger folks usually stay separate, with separate events and separate ministries, even separate pastors attending to our spiritual needs. But a beautiful thing happens in churches when like-minded believers find each other despite their differences in age and season of life.

Our little Foursquare church was so small that on a good day we had six or seven of us at youth group. The other teens who came would show up smelling like cigarette smoke and afterwards would swing by the local convenience store to steal candy. The youth pastor would call the store after youth group to warn the manager that the teens were on their way and should be carefully watched. I was the outlier, with a strong sense of call to missions and a firm commitment to living by the rules. I was eager to get to college and learn Greek so that I could become a Bible translator for an unreached people group. Donna shared that heart, and we found each other. That's the sort of thing that happens in a multigenerational family of faith. We were unlikely companions. I would have missed out on so much if I had only stayed with my peers.

> A beautiful thing happens in churches when like-minded believers find each other despite their differences in age and season of life.

A BIGGER TENT

We began this book with a sneak preview of a momentous event in which the resurrected Jesus instructed his disciples to wait in Jerusalem for the gift of the Holy Spirit (Acts 1:4-5). Their hopes were realized on the day of Pentecost. Unless your church is Anglican, Lutheran, Roman Catholic, or Orthodox, there is a good chance you have never celebrated Pentecost. The actual date varies, but it's always fifty days after Easter. Jesus spent forty days with his disciples after his resurrection, so that means the disciples waited about ten days. To understand the full significance of Pentecost, it helps to know a bit more history.

Remember that Jesus celebrated the Passover with his disciples the night before he died. In Jewish tradition, the annual Passover celebration is followed seven weeks later by the Feast of Weeks, which correlates with the giving of the law at Mount Sinai. It's not hard to see how this tradition developed. Passover was the event that initiated the exodus from Egypt. Some weeks later, the Israelites arrived at Mount Sinai. Centuries later, after the destruction of Israel's second temple, Jews celebrated the Feast of Weeks by reading Ruth, a harvest story, and Exodus 19–20, which celebrates the giving of the law.[9]

In Exodus, Moses ascends the mountain into the presence of God and returns with the law, while in Acts, Jesus ascends into the heavenly presence of God and gives the Spirit. The account of Jesus' ascension includes several echoes of Moses' ascent of Mount Sinai: "forty days," a meal with his delegated leaders, a command to "wait" for a gift, and a "cloud" that hides him from their sight as he ascends (Acts 1:1-9; see Exodus 24:9-18). Clearly, Luke wants us to recognize these similarities. To New Testament scholar Raymond Brown, Acts "presents the Pentecost in Jerusalem as the renewal of God's covenant, once more calling a people to be God's own."[10]

Table 8.1. Parallels between Moses' ascent on Sinai and Jesus' ascension

Moses' Ascent on Sinai (Exodus 24:9-18)	Jesus' Ascension (Acts 1:1-9)
Moses eats with his appointed leaders	Jesus eats with his appointed leaders
Moses commands them to wait	Jesus commands them to wait
Moses says he will "give" the law	Jesus says he will "give" the Spirit
Moses enters the cloud	Jesus enters the cloud
Moses stays away for forty days and nights	Jesus was with them for forty days

During Moses' forty days on Mount Sinai receiving the plans for the tabernacle, the people failed to wait for God's instruction and crafted a golden calf (Exodus 32). Whether they realized it or not, the task for Jesus' disciples while they awaited the gift of the Spirit was to build (become!) a proper temple.[11] The purpose of the law was to facilitate Israel's mission to be a light to the nations. Others should be able to watch Israel to see Yahweh's character and values on display. The prophet Jeremiah envisioned a day when the law would be internalized to make this mission successful: "I will put my law in their minds and write it on their hearts. I will be their God, and they will be my people" (Jeremiah 31:33).

The Holy Spirit was the means for that internalization. As Yahweh said through the prophet Ezekiel, "I will give you a new heart and put a new spirit in you; I will remove from you your heart of stone and give you a heart of flesh. I will put my Spirit in you and move you to follow my decrees and be careful to keep my laws" (Ezekiel 36:26-27). In other words, the Jewish people already had an expectation that someday they would receive the power of the Spirit. It would not replace their original mission to bear God's name among the nations but would rather transform them so they could do it effectively.

Jesus' disciples obey him by staying in Jerusalem. Luke tells us, "They all joined together constantly in prayer, along with the women and Mary the mother of Jesus, and with his brothers" (Acts 1:14). This statement clarifies that the women who followed Jesus were present with the eleven disciples (minus Judas because of his betrayal) and other believers, about 120 in all (Acts 1:15). Together they wait for the Spirit and pray.

The day of Pentecost is the day they've been waiting for. Just as the presence of God came in fire on the tabernacle, on David's altar, and on the temple, so the Spirit descends on each follower of Jesus in the form of flames of fire (Acts 2:3). The fire signals that together, they have become the new temple. The Jerusalem temple is still standing, but when it was rebuilt after the exile, God's fire did not supernaturally appear. By sending fire on the believers—not a fire of judgment that consumed them but a fire that rested lightly on their heads—God indicates the divine decision to dwell among these people who have gathered to pray.

Because the Feast of Weeks was one of the most important Jewish festivals, people from across the Mediterranean world have come to Jerusalem to worship and celebrate. Those gathered include men and women, young and old, from a host of nations. The result of the Spirit's filling is that the followers of Jesus can declare the wonders of God in the languages of all those present (Acts 2:11). Pentecost is not a moment of individual empowerment. The Spirit comes on the gathered community, enabling them to proclaim the gospel to people of other cultural backgrounds.[12] *Together* the early church experiences the power of the Spirit. *Together* they speak in new languages.

Peter interprets this moment for those who have gathered, saying, "God has raised this Jesus to life, and we are all witnesses of it. Exalted to the right hand of God, he has received from the Father the promised Holy Spirit and has poured out what you now see and hear" (Acts 2:32-33).

Anyone can join the movement. All those who repent and are baptized in Jesus' name receive the gift of the Holy Spirit. As Peter explains, "The promise is for you and your children and for all who are far off—for all whom the Lord our God will call" (Acts 2:39). Three thousand people join the movement in one day.

One of my favorite ministry experiences was a summer Vacation Bible School at our church in Oregon City. Our program was a magnet for hundreds of kids from across our city. Every year we transformed our church from top to bottom, creating a full-immersion experience fitting with the theme of VBS. If it was an ocean theme, then the hallways were "underwater," with fish swimming by and octopuses wrapped around doorways and jellyfish suspended from the ceiling. If it was an African safari, the walls became the savannah. Pulling off such a big event required a *lot* of volunteer help. But that's why it was my favorite. The entire church mobilized toward a common goal. Young and old worked side by side, with teen interns deeply invested and families serving together. It was the time of year where we had the most tangible sense that we were a team—that the Spirit had empowered us to do something *together* that none of us could have done alone. We raised money for mission projects one nickel at a time and introduced whole families to the lavish love of God that turns strangers into siblings. I get chills thinking about the sanctuary packed with children, belting out songs about Jesus. We saw no flames descending, but the presence of the Spirit was unmistakable in our midst. It doesn't get better than this.

KEY IDEAS

- Jesus issues a costly call to belong to each other by becoming God's family, a call meant to radically reshape our priorities.
- Jesus is a bridegroom who will return for his bride. If we want union with Christ, we must come together as one.
- To join the Christian community is to join a family. Anyone who does so should be prepared to share their resources accordingly.
- At Pentecost, the Spirit filled the believers who had gathered to pray and wait for God to act, forming a new multilingual and multicultural temple for God's glory.

DIGGING DEEPER

Amy Lindeman Allen. *The Gifts They Bring: How Children in the Gospels Can Shape Inclusive Ministry.* Westminster John Knox, 2023.

Emilio Alvarez. *Pentecost: A Day of Power for All People.* Fullness of Time Series. InterVarsity Press, 2023.

Robbie Castleman. *Parenting in the Pew: Guiding Your Children into the Joy of Worship.* Rev. ed. InterVarsity Press, 2013.

Joseph H. Hellerman. *When the Church Was a Family: Recapturing Jesus' Vision for Authentic Christian Community.* B&H, 2009.

Caryn Reeder. *The Samaritan Woman's Story: Reconsidering John 4 After #ChurchToo.* IVP Academic, 2022.

Kavin Rowe. *World Upside Down: Reading Acts in the Graeco-Roman Age.* Oxford University Press, 2009.

Kaitlyn Scheiss. *Curiously, Kaitlyn* (podcast). Holy Post Media.

Siu Fung Wu. *Finding God in Suffering: Journeying with Jesus and Scriptures.* Wipf & Stock, 2023.

Related videos from BibleProject: "Acts 1–12," "Generosity," and "Anointing."

9

THE FAMILY BUSINESS

BEGINNING WITH THE END

In *Bearing God's Name*, I write about how the list of names in the Old Testament book of Numbers functions like the credits at the end of a movie. We may not even stay to watch them because the names mean nothing to us. Recently I had my first experience at movie theater finding the name of one of my students in the credits. Biola University has a nationally recognized film school, so this won't be the last time it happens. It was a thrill to know that one of our own had been on set, helping bring a great movie to the big screen.

Paul's lists of greetings at the end of most of his letters are a bit like this. We may be tempted to skip them, but these greetings are proof of his theology in action. Scholars today often focus on the concept of justification by faith in Paul's letters, but this doctrine is a standard feature of Old Testament theology and therefore important but not revolutionary. The teaching with real shock value was the new community made possible by the death and resurrection of Christ—a community that dismantled major social barriers to unite people who previously had almost nothing in common. The Old

Testament prophets had looked ahead to this day, but Paul demonstrates that it has become a reality.

In his book, *Reading Romans Backwards*, New Testament scholar Scot McKnight suggests that we can better understand Paul's letter to the Romans by starting at its end. As with most New Testament letters, Paul begins Romans by teaching doctrine and ends with instructions for living. The second half of the book shows us what the doctrine of the first half of the book should look like when we live it out. If we focus on only the first half of the book, interpreting it in isolation from Paul's practical instruction, we may miss the thrust of his letter.

Romans 16 showcases Paul's theology in practice. He begins this grand finale by commending Phoebe to his recipients. She is likely the letter carrier, whose responsibilities included reading and explaining Paul's letter to believers gathered in Rome. Paul highlights her role as deacon of the church and someone whose generosity has funded his ministry. He urges the recipients of his letter to show generous hospitality to her. Phoebe is not merely a courier but one to be received gladly as a sister in Christ. Paul uses sibling language—brother and sister—to reinforce new loyalties to the family of faith.

Paul then extends greetings to twenty-six named individuals and five households or house churches. More accurately, he tells the recipients of his letter to greet each of them, which is a way of accomplishing what he has called them to do. Paul wants to foster mutual respect and gratitude among them. He names eight individuals and "all the churches of Christ" who send greetings with his own (Romans 16:16, 21-24). The list sparkles with Paul's admiration for fellow believers—female and male, young and old, Jews and Gentiles with Hebrew, Greek, and Latin names, some with titles, some without, some who are coworkers of Paul and others whose only qualification seems to be that Paul is fond of them.

One of Paul's favorite designations on this list is "coworker" or those who "work hard" for kingdom purposes. We aren't told what most of them have done, but their essential contributions include hospitality, advocacy, and teaching. Paul does not take their work for granted.

Timothy is one example of someone Paul calls a "co-worker" (Romans 16:21). Timothy is bicultural, with a Greek father and Jewish mother. Paul has taken him under his wing as an apprentice, but Paul doesn't say that here, because he has no need to maintain hierarchy (Acts 16:1). Paul understands himself as part of a family that spans the entire Roman world, including all who have surrendered their lives to Jesus. It's an unlikely coalition, but together they have worked hard, taken risks, suffered, and loved well.

However, not everyone in Rome is a member of this family Paul describes. He warns them to "watch out for those who cause divisions and put obstacles in your way that are contrary to the teaching you have learned" (Romans 16:17). If someone's agenda is to make them suspicious of one another or begin to tear each other down, they should keep their distance. The inclusivity of this community has limits.

After listing all those he wants them to greet, Paul announces, "The God of peace will soon crush Satan under your feet" (Romans 16:20). God announced in the garden of Eden that the seed of the woman would one

> The inclusivity of this community has limits.

day crush the serpent's head (Genesis 3:15). While Jesus' death and resurrection is the clear initial fulfillment of that prophecy, for Paul, the whole sweep of the biblical story finds its climax and fulfillment in the eclectic group of Jesus-followers he addresses in his letter. Jesus conquered sin and death, and they can follow his example by uniting as one to serve Christ (Romans 16:17-18). To crush Satan is not a one-time event. It's part of the ongoing mission of the church.

WOMEN IN MINISTRY WITH PAUL

Church practices must be grounded in the Scriptures. Allowing cultural trends and sensibilities to shift our doctrine is a dangerous and slippery slope. But the trail of biblical faithfulness has a slippery slope on either side. Christian tradition can perpetuate problems if it is not carefully aligned with biblical teaching.

It's understandable that Christians are concerned about shifting cultural values related to gender and sexuality, many of which are at odds with the Bible. Conservatives often attempt to guard against unfaithfulness by doubling down on just two verses in Paul's letters. First Timothy 2:12 and 1 Corinthians 14:35 seem to prohibit women from full participation in gospel ministry. These become paradigm-setting for gender roles in church.

However, we must read *all* that Paul has to say to see the range of ways that women were invited to serve in his ministry. Romans 16 is Exhibit A of the fruitful collaboration that is possible between men and women in ministry. If Paul wanted only men to lead the churches he founded, this would be a prime opportunity to say so. Instead, Paul commends Phoebe, a deacon and benefactor, Priscilla, a teacher of theology, Mary, a hard worker, Junia, an apostle, and many other women who have served alongside him in ministry. Our interpretation of 1 Timothy 2:12 and 1 Corinthians 14:35 must square with Paul's actual practice, which included women in many spiritual leadership roles.

On four occasions, Paul lists spiritual gifts that God grants the church (Romans 12:6-8; 1 Corinthians 12:7-11, 28-31; Ephesians 4:11-13). None of these roles are gendered. Romans and 1 Corinthians describe the gifts as ministry callings given *to* individuals for the sake of the church.[a] If God actively calls both men and women to serve in these capacities, then churches ought to actively encourage women as well as men to fulfill these callings in service to the body. To refuse to do so is to quench the Holy Spirit.

Ephesians 4:11 takes a slightly different approach, and the result is even more poignant. In that letter *people* are the gifts. Apostles, prophets, evangelists, pastors, and teachers are the gifts God gives to the church. Again, Paul makes no gendered distinctions. God provides the church with gifted individuals whose calling is to equip the whole body for works of service and to build up the church in unity and maturity. If we look only to men to fulfill these functions, we may be missing half of God's provision for our spiritual growth. How many of these gifts have been marked "return to sender" by leaders whose parameters for ministry are narrower than Paul's?

First Timothy 2:12 and 1 Corinthians 14:35 are often read too broadly, as if they offer a timeless and universal prohibition of women's contributions to the ministry of the church, even though that interpretation creates contradictions within Paul's own letters. This misreading of Paul is rooted in church tradition rather than Scripture.[b] If women are to remain silent in church, then why doesn't Paul forbid them from praying or prophesying in the public assembly (1 Corinthians 11:5)? Instead, he seems to encourage it. And if women are not to teach the authoritative word of God, why doesn't Paul rebuke Priscilla for teaching Apollos (Acts 18:26), or Philip's daughters for prophesying (Acts 21:9), or Junia for doing whatever apostolic ministry it was that got her arrested and jailed (Romans 16:7)? Instead, Paul says he is unconcerned about who preaches as long as Christ is proclaimed (Philippians 1:12-19). He regards himself as "an apostle—sent not by men nor by a man but by Jesus Christ and God the Father who raised him from the dead" (Galatians 1:1). In other words, for Paul the ultimate Caller is God, not church leaders.

EATING TOGETHER

If we read Romans backward, chapter 16 sets the stage for the kind
of churches Paul commends—those marked by collaboration in
ministry from a wide variety of people, including both men and
women. Scot McKnight is convinced that Paul's instructions about
the "strong" and the "weak" in Romans 14–15 are central to Paul's
mission. If believers are going to be successful in establishing
churches that include everyone—Jew and Gentile, slave and free,
male and female, social elites and outsiders—then they will need to
be able to navigate the inevitable social tensions that will result.
McKnight explains,

> In the providential plans of God, the church was the Body of
> Christ that expanded Israel's borders to include gentiles in the
> one true family of God under the world's one true Lord, King
> Jesus. Paul observed tensions between what he here calls the
> Weak and the Strong in each mission community he established.
> His fear was denominations—one Jewish, one gentile—and
> his message was peace among the Weak and the Strong.[1]

Given the way Paul ends Romans 15 with Old Testament quotations
about Gentile inclusion, it's likely that the strong and the weak primarily (though not exclusively) divide along ethnic lines.[2] The weak
are primarily Jewish believers in Jesus who strictly adhere to Torah
observance, while the strong are primarily Gentile believers who
express religious zeal without reference to the Torah. The two groups
have divergent ideas about what life should look like for followers
of Jesus. That makes it difficult to gather around the same table.
Mealtimes are fraught with controversy because the strong eat anything, but the weak feel it is important to make sure the food preparation complies with Torah regulations or at least that it has not been
offered to idols as a sacrifice. Paul concludes, "Let us therefore make

every effort to do what leads to peace and to mutual edification. Do not destroy the work of God for the sake of food" (Romans 14:19-20).

We might not have the same struggles today as the early church (although some messianic believers still feel strongly today about following Torah regulations regarding food, and this issue divides some families and congregations). We are more likely to divide over political parties or cultural movements such as Black Lives Matter, immigration reform, the appropriate way to engage questions of sexual identity, whether Christians can or should drink alcohol, what women are allowed to do in church, which Bible translation is best, or what style of music is best suited for corporate worship. But Paul's message for us today is just as urgent. According to McKnight, "The central action of Christian ethics for Paul in Romans is welcome."[3]

Paul's vision is a dinner table where we pursue people who are not like us with the goal of becoming knit together as family. What if the goal of our social calendar were to eat with people who think differently than we do? What sort of world would this be if we moved toward those whose views challenge our own rather than moving away from them?

We tend to characterize others according to what we *don't* share. Person A (let's say that's me) feels like their views are totally incompatible with Person B. We seem to have irreconcilable differences.

But if we map out our views on a wider variety of topics, rather than just one hot-button

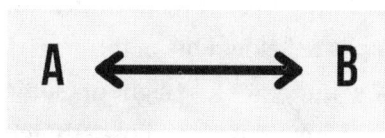

Figure 9.1. Opposing perspectives

issue, look how much we have in common (see Figure 9.2). To see Person B as an adversary ignores the many areas of overlap in life experience and perspective that we share.

These days it's common to talk about "finding your people." If you move to a new city or join a new community (say, a university, or a

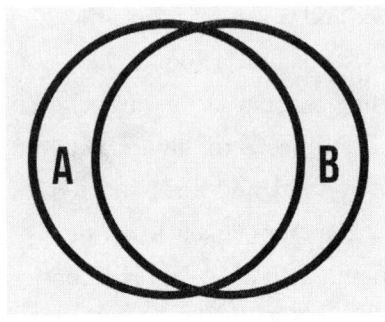

Figure 9.2. Shared perspectives

recreation center, or new workplace), it can take time to find the people with whom you feel most at home. We've lived in Southern California for three years now. Partly because of the pace of life here, it has taken longer than usual to develop friendships. Finding like-minded people requires patience and perseverance. But looking for people just like us can be a form of idolatry.

Not long ago, I received an email invitation to participate in a project. My immediate internal response was, "Those aren't my people." The Holy Spirit firmly but gently convicted me over the next few hours. "Carmen, those are *my* people." While we may disagree on certain doctrinal points or matters of church practice, those who had extended the invitation were unquestionably part of the family of faith. That made them my siblings in Christ.

Our natural inclination is to sort ourselves into smaller and smaller communities made up of people who think just like we do. Social media algorithms facilitate this process. Forming homogeneous communities is even a church-planting strategy in some circles, as we'll see below. One of the great dangers in sorting ourselves in this way is that we lose sight of God's purpose to form a diverse family made up of people whose ethnicity, social standing, education, gender, and gifting make a unique contribution to the whole. We often have more common ground than we think. The smaller and more uniform our circle of friends, the more likely we are to exaggerate our differences with those who are outside our immediate group.

Paul has no patience for factions. The true family of faith is marked by hospitality. God calls us to arrange our lives so that we have room for others. As Marva Dawn explains, "Hospitality cannot be given merely by contributions to charities. It requires giving of myself—my time, my energy, my home, my friendship, my faith, my resources, my whole self."[4]

For the church in Rome, the singular challenge to obeying God was the difficulty believers had in meeting together peacefully. Their different ethnic backgrounds gave rise to diverse priorities and values. It was much easier to stick with their tribes—sharing life with those whose language, class, diet, culture, and ethnicity aligned with their own. But to do that would miss the very heart of the gospel. The whole point of Christian fellowship was to celebrate and enjoy the peace *between* these factions that Christ had accomplished through his death and resurrection. They'd each been adopted into a new family. Paul would never be content as long as members of God's family were estranged from one another. Avoidance of those who don't look like us or think like we do is much easier than engagement, but it misses some of the greatest gifts God offers through the church.

ONE BODY

One church-planting strategy that has enjoyed popularity over the past forty years is known as the homogeneous unit principle.[5] The idea is to start churches that appeal to a very small subset of the population who share a lot in common, such as young Black urban professionals with no kids, or White suburban families, or second-generation immigrants from Central America. According to proponents of the homogeneous unit principle, targeting micro-demographics is the fastest way to grow a church. And they're right. Creating communities of individuals who are alike is not difficult.

The problem is that the homogeneous unit principle ignores the New Testament vision for churches that radically challenge the status quo. In the first century, believers defied cultural norms by eating together across the typical divides of class, gender, and ethnicity. Paul's letters to the churches at Ephesus and Corinth are clear about the need for believers to reject segregated gatherings.

Churches formed around similar demographics allow believers to remain unaware of the needs of others and of their own needs for the contribution of others. Worshiping in an echo chamber breeds ethnocentrism, consumerism, and classism. Hanging out with people who are just like me reinforces my life choices and allows my perspectives to go uncontested.

According to Paul's letter to the Ephesians, to be reconciled to Christ requires reconciliation to one another. The New Testament uses a variety of metaphors to talk about the church. We are Christ's body, Christ's bride, members of God's household, fellow citizens, and a new temple of the Spirit. What these metaphors all have in common is unity. Christ has only one body, one bride, one temple, one household, one kingdom. As we are united to Christ, we are united to one another.

For us to experience Christian maturity, we must embrace one another. In Paul's words, "His purpose was to create in himself one new humanity out of the two, thus making peace, and in one body to reconcile both of them to God through the cross, by which he put to death their hostility" (Ephesians 2:15-16).

We have already discussed how churches should be multicultural and embrace the ministries of both men and women. How can we overcome class divisions? In his recent book, *Christ Among the Classes*, Al Tizon challenges the rich to embrace simplicity, compassion, generosity, hospitality, friendship, and solidarity with the poor.[6] (You may not *feel* rich, but the reality is that the world's poor could never

> Christ has only one body, one bride, one temple, one household, one kingdom. As we are united to Christ, we are united to one another.

hope to buy and read a book of their own or even access one in a library.)

Tizon's challenge echoes that of René Padilla and Samuel Escobar, who addressed the first Lausanne Congress on World Evangelization in 1974 with a prophetic call for the Western, American church to recognize its cultural captivity. The church often falls prey to the values of the world, refusing to question unbiblical values such as consumer lifestyles and the pursuit of pleasure. The Western church often assumes it has the corner on the market of gospel ministry, with everything to give the world and nothing to learn from it. Many churches in the United States uncritically accept the ideas that bigger is better, that technology leads to excellence, that personal needs come before group needs, and that might makes right. By mimicking worldly values, we miss out on the empowerment of the Spirit for transformational ministry.

René Padilla credits Brian McLaren with saying, "We don't recruit people to be customers of our products or consumers of our religious programs; we recruit them to be colleagues in our mission. The church does not exist in order to satisfy the consumer demands of believers; the church exists to equip and mobilise men and women for God's mission in the world."[7] We need someone outside ourselves to hold up a mirror to our lives by telling us what they see. The global church can bear prophetic witness to the theological distortions of the American church (and vice versa!), helping us to perceive the ways we have absorbed the values of our culture rather than embodied gospel values. Padilla laments that the American church has become so worldly that it has lost "the capacity . . . to denounce the social evils in its own situation," going so far as "to integrate racial and class segregation into its strategy for world evangelization."[8] This is the legacy of the homogeneous unit principle.

The need to listen to critique from marginalized groups remains urgent. To sit around the same table with those whose backgrounds are unlike our own can be messy. We will not always see things eye to eye. But we must keep drawing up our chairs and seeking to understand. Too often the call for unity drowns out the perspectives of others.

For many, the problem is not hostility toward people of other cultures or classes but apathy or pride. It is difficult to imagine that someone from another background has something to offer me that I need. However, Paul sees us as fellow members of the body of Christ.

> Too often the call for unity drowns out the perspectives of others.

He writes, "From him the whole body, joined and held together by every supporting ligament, grows and builds itself up in love, as each part does its work" (Ephesians 4:16). To reject another or to withhold ourselves from the body is to impoverish the community. Paul writes, "To each one the manifestation of the Spirit is given for the common good" (1 Corinthians 12:7). I am not my own. I belong to you. You belong to me. We need each other to truly flourish and become the mature Christian community among which God's presence is manifest to the world.

WHEN TO LEAVE A CHURCH

Is it ever right to leave a church? My husband and I have wrestled with this question multiple times over the years. While my list is not the final word on the subject, in my view, the following three scenarios indicate that it's time to leave:

First, a church that has lost its foundation in the Word of God cannot sustain a faithful community of Jesus-followers. This does *not* mean that if you disagree with something your pastor says you ought to leave. I'm not suggesting that we leave over different *interpretations* of Scripture. Scripture contains so many mysteries that we will never see things entirely eye to eye. It's normal for us to experience some disagreement. However, if a church no longer considers Scripture its foundation, the congregation is in grave danger. If the Bible has become an outdated catalog of ancient ideas or cannot be trusted to help navigate moral quandaries today, then it's time to find a new church.

The second and third reasons for leaving are related. If a church has a toxic leadership culture in which those in leadership refuse to listen to members of the congregation who raise valid concerns or if they ignore the need for every member to serve, that is another good reason to leave. Authoritarian leadership styles can foster abuses of many kinds—including spiritual, physical, and sexual abuse. The purpose of a church is not to provide a platform for a narcissistic leader to gain followers or control others. Godly leaders lead people to Jesus, not to themselves. They are honest about their limitations, repentant of their sin, grateful for God's grace, and serious about every member of the body serving others. Above all, if you have experienced abuse in your church or are aware of others who have, and if church leadership has not taken those allegations seriously, it's time to leave.

Aside from these three situations—rejection of scriptural authority, authoritarian leadership, or abusive behavior that is not properly addressed—we should be very hesitant to leave a church. Scripture asks us to treat other believers as family, even when we disagree or have different preferences about what happens when we gather. If God's goal is to bring people together from different walks of life who will become God's family to one another, then we only hinder God's mission when we hop from place to place trying to find people who look and think exactly like we do.

If you find yourself in a situation where you must leave, commit to finding another church. We are not meant to walk alone. We are members of God's family, built together to be a dwelling for the Spirit.

WHO'S IN? WHO'S OUT?

Romans 9–11 is often held up as the center of Paul's theology. People think of it as an academic treatise on election—the doctrine of who is saved and how God selected those individuals and not others. However, if we read these chapters in context, as aiming toward the practical implications in Romans 12–16, we can see more clearly that Paul's aim is not to talk about individual salvation but rather mutual acceptance. Paul intends to show that Gentile inclusion in God's family is consistent with God's original covenant promises to Abraham. He's thinking in terms of groups—Israelites and Gentiles—not individuals.

Paul famously says, "All Israel will be saved" (Romans 11:26), but to understand his point we must carefully consider how he has defined his terms. Here I'm relying on Jason Staples's book *Paul and the Resurrection of Israel*. Staples notes that Paul uses the word *Israel* only six times in his other letters and never in Romans outside Romans 9–11, compared to thirteen times in these chapters.[9] Usually Paul refers to "the Jews," a term that appears twenty-nine times elsewhere in his letters but only twice in Romans 9–11. The frequency alone should alert us to the fact that Paul is up to something different here. *Jews* and *Israel* are *not* synonymous.

Technically speaking, the Jews are descendants of the Southern Kingdom of Judah, those affected by the Babylonian exile in the sixth century BCE. Israel, on the other hand, includes the ten tribes of the Northern Kingdom who were deported and scattered by the Assyrians two hundred years prior. A major concern in Jewish literature leading up to the first century CE was that the northern tribes had not yet been restored from exile. Because Israel was deported and scattered, the northern tribes lost their ethnic identity through assimilation to the nations. In a sense, those tribes died out. The dramatic announcement Paul makes in Romans 9–11 is that God's promises regarding the restoration of all Israel will be fulfilled *through the incorporation of believing Gentiles from among those nations.*

By this point in Paul's letter to the Romans, he has already clarified that "A person is not a Jew who is one only outwardly. . . . No, a person is a Jew who is one inwardly" (Romans 2:28-29). Even Jews, some of whose lineage could be traced back with confidence to the preexilic period, do not qualify as covenant members unless they have maintained faithfulness to the covenant. Covenant membership is grounded not in ethnicity but faithfulness to God. That perspective opens the door for an alternative way of thinking about Israel. In Paul's words, "Not all who are descended from Israel are Israel" (Romans 9:6), and "Not all the Israelites accepted the good news" (Romans 10:16). Only those who receive the covenant promises by faith—as expressed in Jesus the Messiah—constitute the faithful remnant. Paul begins saying this early in his letter to clarify that the way is open for others to join the covenant people.

The surprising mystery is that God welcomes Gentile participation in the Abrahamic covenant along with believing Jews. The two peoples do not have a separate path to salvation: "There is no difference between Jew and Gentile—the same Lord is Lord of all and richly blesses all who call on him" (Romans 10:12). Believing Gentiles also do not *replace* the people of Israel. According to Staples, because the tribes of the Northern Kingdom were all but lost among the nations, the fulfillment of God's promises regarding the restoration of Israel depends on gathering Gentile followers of Jesus from among those nations. Their inclusion in the family of faith constitutes the resurrection of Israel from the dead.

This radical reconfiguration of the covenant family requires a significant change in practice. For Paul, to "conform to the pattern of this world" (Romans 12:2) is to continue to live with deep divisions between Jewish and Gentile believers in Jesus. God announces a new way forward for the family of faith: together we "form one body" (Romans 12:5) and must be "devoted to one another in love" (Romans 12:10).

BECOMING ONE

The difficulty of becoming God's family across ethnic and racial divisions has not dissipated since the first century. It remains one of the areas of greatest struggle in the church today. Some Christians in the United States are concerned that an influx of newcomers from around the world will result in the church having less and less of a voice in our culture. Growing numbers of Muslims or Buddhists in America sometimes makes White Protestants suspicious of all people of color. However, Soong Chan-Rah points out that the rise of immigration and the declining numbers of people of White European descent has not resulted in a decline in Christianity.[10] On the contrary, Christianity is flourishing among non-Whites. Most of our nation's church growth today is among people of color, especially immigrants. To welcome people from other countries may be the best way to ensure the future of the church in America.

We can celebrate the growth in cultural and ethnic diversity as a taste of heaven. We can thank our brothers and sisters around the world for holding fast to the truth of Scripture. According to the Bible, we'll be spending eternity in the new creation with people from every ethnic group, language, and nation.

> Most of our nation's church growth today is among people of color, especially immigrants. To welcome people from other countries may be the best way to ensure the future of the church in America.

Not long after my husband and I married, we joined a rural Mennonite church where his grandfather had pastored in the 1970s (the church with the Women's Missionary Society I wrote about earlier). Our

A-frame sanctuary was surrounded by tree farms and plant nurseries. The congregation was aging; many of their children had moved to the city for work.

In the mid-'90s, the pastor invited a couple to start worship services in Spanish in the education building. The two churches arranged a combined Sunday school in English for the children. Back when we attended, now and then the two congregations would hold a joint potluck or other community event. Ten years later, when we returned after serving overseas and elsewhere as missionaries, a transformation had occurred.

The Spanish-speaking congregation had grown significantly. Their rented room was no longer large enough for their services. Meanwhile, the English-speaking congregation had continued to decline in numbers. The children of both groups who had grown up together were part of the bond that resulted in an official merger of the two churches, complete with a new church covenant and copastors.

We were delighted to find that weekly worship was bilingual, often led by the youth who had grown up together, and that sermons alternated between English and Spanish, along with worship songs. During a recent visit, Pastor Kevin led Communion in English with Spanish translation, and we listened to Pastor Victor preach in Spanish with English translation on our headsets. What a beautiful thing to see two groups becoming one! The church is not uniform, but they are united in Christ.

The process of merging has not been easy. Both groups have had to adjust, laying down their need to have things "their way" all the time. However, by using both languages in the services, each community retains its cultural distinctiveness. They show genuine hospitality to one another, discovering a richer and wider experience of friendship in God's presence. To me it offers a glimpse of the new creation.

John's vision in the book of Revelation points to the reconstitution
of the people of God on multiple levels. His revelation from Jesus
includes letters to seven churches, the number of completeness
(Revelation 1–3). God's throne room features twenty-four elders,
symbolizing the twelve tribes and twelve others, perhaps to reflect
the inclusion of the nations (Revelation 4:4, 9-11). Those marked
with God's name on their foreheads number 144,000—twelve thousand from each tribe—indicating the full restoration of the lost tribes
of Israel through the inclusion of the nations (Revelation 7:1-8; see
Revelation 7:9-12).[11]

Notably, John's vision of God's throne room includes corporate,
multiethnic worship. The elders around the throne of God sing to
the Lamb, who represents Jesus, saying, "You are worthy to take the
scroll and to open its seals, because you were slain, and with your
blood you purchased for God *persons from every tribe and language
and people and nation. You have made them to be a kingdom and
priests to serve our God, and they will reign on the earth*" (Revelation 5:9-10, emphasis added). Given the exclusivity of the Roman
Empire and its privileged place for those of Roman descent, the
Bible's multiethnic vision is striking. According to Rome, Jewish
people would always be outsiders (e.g., Acts 18:2). Paul's status as a
Roman citizen surprised Roman leaders for precisely that reason
(Acts 22:25-29).

Our future vocation extends our current occupation: to serve
God side by side with people from around the globe, bearing witness
to the kingship of Yahweh, who is Creator and Redeemer of all things,
while we wait and groan and pray for Christ's kingdom to come fully
on earth. As I've said before, this is a group project. Our future is
neither aimed at individual happiness nor centered on our biological
families. By faith in Christ, we enter the ultimate royal family, with
whom we carry out our collective mission, oriented toward the return

of Christ and built together into a new temple where the Spirit dwells. *That's* what it means to be a Christian.

KEY IDEAS

- The most groundbreaking feature of Paul's message was the new community made possible by the death and resurrection of Christ—a community that united people who previously had almost nothing in common.

- Paul commended women who served in a wide variety of roles in the church, including teaching, giving, leading, prophesying, and working hard in ministry.

- Avoidance of those who don't look like us or think like we do is much easier than engagement, but it misses some of the greatest gifts God offers through the church.

- The fulfillment of God's promises regarding the restoration of Israel depends on gathering Gentile followers of Jesus from among the nations.

- Christ only has one body, one bride, one temple, one household, one kingdom. As we are united to Christ, we are united to one another.

DIGGING DEEPER

Kenneth Berding. *What Are Spiritual Gifts? Rethinking the Conventional View.* Kregel, 2006.

Sandra Glahn. *Nobody's Mother: Artemis of the Ephesians in Antiquity and the New Testament.* IVP Academic, 2023.

Nijay Gupta. *Tell Her Story: How Women Led, Taught, and Ministered in the Early Church.* IVP Academic, 2023.

Joseph H. Hellerman. *When the Church Was a Family: Recapturing Jesus' Vision for Authentic Christian Community.* B&H, 2009.

Carmen Joy Imes. "'Your Sons and Daughters Will Prophesy': Healing the Body of Christ by Restoring a Biblical Vision of

Spirit Empowerment." *Journal of Spiritual Formation and Soul Care* (Fall 2024).

Christa L. McKirland. *A Theology of Authority: Rethinking Leadership in the Church.* Baker Academic, 2025.

Scot McKnight. *Reading Romans Backwards: A Gospel of Peace in the Midst of Empire.* Baylor University Press, 2019.

Jason A. Staples. *Paul and the Resurrection of Israel: Jews, Former Gentiles, Israelites.* Cambridge University Press, 2024.

N. T. Wright. *Into the Heart of Romans: A Deep Dive into Paul's Greatest Letter.* Zondervan Academic, 2023.

Related videos from BibleProject: "Romans 1–4" and "The Last Will Be First."

10

A NEW TEMPLE

FINDING TRUE NORTH

Perhaps at this point in our journey together, you are thinking, "OK, Carmen. I get your point. The church matters. The ideal is to gather regularly with a diverse group of Jesus-followers to pray and wait for his second coming. But practically speaking, it just doesn't work for me or my family. Our weeks are crazy busy. Our schedule is full to the brim. We've got sports on Sunday mornings, and we're often traveling. And when we're home, what we need most is a quiet morning to sleep in. I connect with God best when I have a cup of coffee and a good sermon on YouTube or time to read Scripture on my own."

If that describes you, I hope this book has given you a taste of what you might be missing. Yes, it takes work to organize our lives to make room to participate in the family of faith, but the rewards are great. Consider this your invitation to reimagine the next season. It may involve cutting back on other commitments to make room for church.

I think of a weekly church service like the calibration of a magnetic compass. A compass indicates true north by responding to the magnetic pull of the North Pole. But a compass can get out of alignment if it gets too close to other magnets or electronic equipment. Even a metal object can corrupt a compass. The needle can become sluggish or even reverse completely. For a compass to work properly, it must be remagnetized or calibrated regularly.

Our inner compass is designed to point to God and God's wisdom as our true north. However, the world is full of magnetic distractions large and small that pull us off center and seek to redefine our values. We may not learn anything new on a Sunday morning. (Learning is not the primary goal of a worship gathering anyway.) We may not witness anything that seems dramatic or profound. But beneath the surface, if a church is healthy and worship is genuine, the habit of gathering calibrates our compass, keeping us on the path that helps us walk faithfully with God and with one another. Worship shapes our affections.

James K. A. Smith attributes this transformation to an encounter with God. He explains, "Historic Christian worship is rooted in the conviction that God is the primary actor or agent in the worship encounter. . . . Worship is the arena in which God recalibrates our hearts, reforms our desires, and rehabituates our loves. Worship isn't just something we do; it is where God does something *to* us." We might have assumed that the main characteristic of a Christian would be a certain set of beliefs. Smith insists that Christian faith has more to do with desires. "Discipleship is more a matter of hungering and thirsting than of knowing and believing."[1] When we gather regularly to wait for God, our desire for his presence grows while other, less important desires, shrink to their proper size.

When we moved to Southern California from a small town in Alberta, we knew we'd be near the center of the entertainment industry. We felt the tension between an opportunity to disciple Christian students who could contribute to that industry and the dangers of absorbing worldly values uncritically. Doing theology in the shadow of Hollywood or Disneyland requires vigilance lest we conform too much to our environment.

On our way to our new home, we passed a shopping mall that made my jaw drop. Right in the thick of the greater Los Angeles area, next to Interstate 5, is a mall intentionally styled after a Babylonian temple. Giant lamassu figurines (bulls with human heads and wings) stand at attention, looking out over the freeway. A ziggurat in the center features stone artwork of the king of Babylon approaching the deity.

The design is merely a facade—once you leave the freeway and enter the mall, the Babylonian imagery disappears, replaced by the stores and restaurants you would expect to see. However, the symbolism is not as far-fetched as it may seem. In Scripture, Babylon becomes the archetype of worldly powers and the ultimate enemy of the people of God. In this present day, one of the greatest threats to our participation in the family of faith is the siren call of the world to acquire more for ourselves and to enrich our lifestyles so that we become like the rich and famous we see on screen. Becoming God's family involves rejecting these worldly priorities.

Smith warns that shopping malls are the temples of our generation, seeking to inspire awe and gather people for the purpose of spending money.[2] The transcendence we feel in a shopping mall offers a cheap alternative to the transcendence of cathedrals built

> Becoming God's family involves rejecting worldly priorities.

for worship. The "secular liturgies" of shopping and spending beckon us to "the good life." However, the version of the good life advertised in shopping malls is a far cry from the path to true flourishing found in the family of faith. The Christian faith is not an optional extracurricular activity that provides an outlet for stress or enriches the cultivation of higher thoughts. Reading the New Testament should easily disabuse us of this notion. True faith involves an entirely new worldview and set of values. As the gospel spread throughout the Roman Empire, it called for a radical break with the prevailing culture and its rush to acquire more wealth, honor, or power.

As we discussed earlier, the sequence of stories in Acts 14–19 in Lystra, Philippi, Athens, and Ephesus demonstrates the profound incompatibility between Christian and pagan ways of life. Paul's message disrupted the economy, provoked legal disputes, and caused riots. In short, early Christianity was not a movement in which anyone was welcome without judgment. The Christian message was a force for "cultural destabilization."[3] It still is.

Is it any wonder that the author of Hebrews wants us to keep meeting? "Let us consider how we may spur one another on toward love and good deeds, *not giving up meeting together, as some are in the habit of doing*, but encouraging one another—and all the more as you see the Day approaching" (Hebrews 10:24-25, emphasis added). "The Day" that Hebrews speaks about is the day of the Lord, the long-awaited return of God to judge the wicked and vindicate the righteous. A community oriented toward that day is one whose ethical commitments are formed by a proper fear of God, recognizing his ultimate authority and rule. Churches that live in eager expectation of God's return are less likely to be distracted by the latest trends.

Hebrews uses a strong word to encourage believers to keep meeting. Amy Peeler's translation reads, "not deserting the gathering." Peeler explains, "The word for 'deserting' has a more intense meaning than 'forgetting' or 'neglecting.' It conveys . . . an active desertion."[4] Attridge translates it as "wrongful abandonment."[5] Surely, we can extend this warning to those whose neglect is less deliberate. It takes energy to commit to the family of believers, just as it takes energy to maintain the health and commitment of a marriage or a friendship.

FACING EAST

Christine Caine spoke in chapel at Biola University about the Christian
life using the analogy of sailing. She said, "All it takes to drift is . . .
nothing." If we don't aim our sails so that they catch the wind of the
Spirit by joining a faith community, we will naturally drift from biblical
faithfulness and deep connection with each other. It takes work not to.
Our boat, like our compass, can easily lose sight of our destination.

The temple in Jerusalem was anchored to the spot where God's
fire had fallen on David's altar. The temple faced east, permanently
oriented in the direction of God's expected return. Jesus fulfilled
those expectations in his first coming when he rode into Jerusalem
on a donkey from the Mount of Olives, directly east of the old city
of Jerusalem.

The author of Hebrews devotes a great deal of time to demonstrating that the earthly temple was merely a shadow of the real temple
in the heavenly realm. Those earthly symbols—the temple, the sacrifices, and the high priest—all pointed ahead to the rock-solid reality
of Christ's sacrifice and Christ's priestly work that secured believers'
entrance into God's most holy presence. In other words, our participation in the church connects us with something more real than
what we can see with our eyes. The day of Pentecost pointed to this
reality when the fire of God's Spirit rested visibly on believers, signi-
fying that the gathered people of God constituted the new temple.

Hebrews turns from that deep truth to its practical implications.
Family imagery is front and center: "Therefore, brothers and sisters,
since we have confidence to enter the Most Holy Place by the blood
of Jesus . . . let us draw near to God . . . let us hold unswervingly to
the hope we profess . . . and let us consider how we may spur one
another on" (Hebrews 10:19, 22-24). What emerges from the fresh
access to the presence of God provided by Jesus is our family status.
The natural outcome of drawing near to God is meeting with one

another for mutual encouragement. The Christian life was never meant to be solitary.

Participating in a church community is not an extracurricular activity for those who want to be super-Christians. Instead, church participation is the central means by which every Christian becomes part of God's family and participates in God's kingdom. We express our God-given vocation by serving the community in accordance with God's calling—not to earn a place in God's family but to enjoy belonging. When we don't show up, some of God's gifts intended for the benefit of others are missing.

> Church participation is the central means by which every Christian becomes part of God's family and participates in God's kingdom.

The author of Hebrews calls the neglect of meeting with fellow believers a "habit" for some. A habit is something that no longer requires a decision because it has become second nature. If the default on a Sunday morning (or Saturday for some) is something *other* than church attendance, then the energy required to overcome that habit on any given week is high.

However, if church attendance is a habit, we don't even have to ask the question, "Are we going to church this week?" We simply organize our lives accordingly. The question is not, "Do we have time to go to church this weekend?" but rather, "What are we going to do with the time we have left?" We don't ask, "Will it be worth it to stay connected to this community?" The Bible has already insisted that we are defined by membership in God's family. We're not in a position to see the ultimate impact of that decision. We come in obedience, trusting that the Spirit works as we gather.

It's easy to assume that if I don't show up at church, no one will notice. But something mysterious and powerful happens when we are present with one another. We've seen so many examples of this on the pages of Scripture—evidence that God's presence dwells among his people.

We need one another more desperately than we realize. Theologian Christa McKirland argues that God created humanity with a fundamental need for a personal relationship with God, such that we cannot flourish without it.[6] Whether or not we recognize this need, it is our fundamental disposition. Sin disrupts the satisfaction of this need because it distances us from God.

Humans also have a fundamental need for communion with one another. A community gathered around God's indwelling presence recognizes its dependence on him and the ways he meets our collective needs through each other. This book is about the community God is forming around himself as a dwelling of the Spirit—a family in which our relation to God also entails a bond with one another. Without you, I cannot follow Jesus in all the ways I'm meant to. We cannot experience union with Christ without also pursuing and receiving union with others.

The kind of neighbor love expected of Christ-followers is best expressed when we spend time with other people and find out their needs. When we moved into our current neighborhood, we began walking to church. Often, we'd see Mike sitting out on his driveway in a lawn chair or waxing one of his classic cars. I didn't walk over and invite him to join us, but we always waved and said hello. I prayed that Mike would encounter Jesus. Now and then, on our walks around the block, we'd stop to chat.

> This book is about the community God is forming around himself as a dwelling of the Spirit—a family in which our relation to God also entails a bond with one another.

One day, Mike showed up in church. He sat in the back row, and he kept coming back week after week. To say that I was thrilled would be an understatement. Having him there gave us a natural opportunity to talk about spiritual things. On several occasions, he asked questions that he'd been wondering about the Bible or Christian theology. One day he told me he was ready to be baptized, and he wanted me to do it. Just think what I would have missed out on if I'd stayed at home.

LINKING LEGO BRICKS

Another analogy about the church will drive this point home. One LEGO brick by itself is neither beautiful nor useful. And anyone who has stepped on one in bare feet can tell you that a solitary LEGO can be downright dangerous! LEGO bricks are designed to be attached to other LEGO bricks. A whole pile of LEGO bricks, fitted together with care and creativity, can become something truly impressive.

This is how Peter sees the church. His first letter uses a variety of metaphors. He calls the believers scattered throughout Asia Minor "God's elect," "exiles," "obedient children," "newborn babies," "a chosen people, a royal priesthood, a holy nation, God's special possession," "the people of God," "God's household," "God's flock," and the "family of believers" (1 Peter 1:1, 14; 2:2, 9-10; 4:17; 5:2, 9). Another metaphor he uses is particularly striking: Peter imagines believers as

Figure 10.1. A single LEGO brick

"living stones . . . being built into a spiritual house" (1 Peter 2:5). Each believer is like a single LEGO brick, designed to connect with other LEGO bricks to form a new temple. Jesus himself is the cornerstone. Alone, we cannot fulfill our purpose.

Paul makes the same point when he writes to the Ephesians: "Consequently, you are no longer foreigners and strangers, but fellow citizens with God's people and also members of his household, built on the foundation of the apostles and prophets, with Christ Jesus himself as the chief cornerstone. In him the whole building, being joined together, grows into a holy temple in the Lord" (Ephesians 2:19-21). On our own, any one of us is incomplete. We are meant to join with others to become something more than we can be by ourselves. We gather prayerfully, serving one another and waiting for God to act among us. God chooses *this* community in which to tabernacle and to manifest his presence to the world. (Visit www.ivpress.com/imes94 for a cool LEGO temple!)

John warns, "Anyone who claims to be in the light but hates a brother or sister is still in the darkness" (1 John 2:9). We need to examine our attitudes toward each other regularly. Who are my brothers and sisters in the Lord? Am I loving them well? Or have I sorted them into categories of those who deserve my friendship and those who don't? John does not mince words. He boldly writes, "This is how we know who the children of God are and who the children of the devil are: Anyone who does not do what is right is not God's child, *nor is anyone who does not love their brother and sister*" (1 John 3:10).

Paul's family commitment is evident in the fondness he exhibits for fellow believers.[7] Paul's letter to the Thessalonian church shows deep attachment to them:

> Brothers and sisters, when we were orphaned by being separated from you for a short time (in person, not in thought), out of our intense longing we made every effort to see you. For we wanted to come to you—certainly I, Paul, did, again and again—but Satan blocked our way. For what is our hope, our joy, or the crown in which we will glory in the presence of our Lord Jesus when he comes? Is it not you? Indeed, you are our glory and joy. (1 Thessalonians 2:17-20)

Our doctrine may be precise and our church-planting methods sound, but if we don't *like* the people in our church, they will not entrust themselves to us, nor we to them. Paul models fondness in so many ways as he longs to be with those with whom he has shared the gospel. He is so distraught over his separation from those in Thessalonica that he feels "orphaned" during their separation. It takes time to develop this level of connection with people outside our biological family, but Paul makes it a high priority. So should we.

> Our doctrine may be precise and our church-planting methods sound, but if we don't *like* the people in our church, they will not entrust themselves to us, nor we to them.

If we're one body in Christ, then what happens to you affects me and vice versa. Paul insists, "If one part suffers, every part suffers with it; if one part is honored, every part rejoices with it" (1 Corinthians 12:26). An ingrown toenail may be small, but the pain can be debilitating. When we treat one another as members of one body, we take on one another's struggles as our own.

To share in the sufferings of others is part of what it means to become God's family. According to Romans 8:22-27, God sends us as he sent Jesus—straight into the pain of the world, to groan alongside creation as we await God's restoration of all things.[8] N. T. Wright calls this the heart of the gospel in Romans. Surprisingly, it's not a vocation of victory and celebration but of groaning and lament. He explains, "Part of our primary calling as followers of Jesus is to lament: to stand in the place of pain in humility, sorrow and hope."[9]

This commitment comes with very practical implications. Paul leverages family language for a project very near and dear to his heart: fundraising efforts in Corinth for impoverished Jewish believers in Jerusalem. As Joseph Hellerman explains, "Jew and Gentile are now siblings in God's eternal family, and alleviating a brother's poverty is, first and foremost, a family responsibility."[10] By encouraging generosity toward fellow believers, Paul hopes to cultivate broader unity between Jewish and Gentile followers of Jesus. Meeting financial needs is one way to demonstrate unity.

If we want to become part of God's family, we have no choice but to embrace our siblings and learn how to love each another—laying down our lives for one another and sharing with those in need (1 John 3:16-18). John expresses the theme we have been exploring in this book when he speaks of God's indwelling presence: "Dear friends, since God so loved us, we also ought to love one another. No one has ever seen God; but *if we love one another, God lives in us and his love is made complete in us*" (1 John 4:11-12).

The preposition *in* could also be translated "among," though all the English translations I checked read "in." Perhaps our translations are the fruit of Western individuality. The sentence more naturally reads, "God lives *among* us and his love is made complete *among* us." If we want to experience the presence and love of God, we must move toward each other. Like LEGO bricks connected to other LEGO bricks, together we become the temple of God.

A WORD TO CHRISTIAN COLLEGE STUDENTS

I realize that many people reading this book will not be college students. For those who are, I would like to make a case for why chapel services on a college campus should not replace church attendance. Certainly, a church service and a chapel service overlap in certain ways. Singing worship songs, hearing a message, even seeing other believers and sharing the experience with them—these aspects are similar. However, as valuable as chapel can be, it is no substitute for church. More happens on a Sunday morning than singing and teaching and fellowship.

In church, we take Communion together, remembering what Christ has done to make us one. We witness baptisms—an initiation rite in which someone becomes a member of our faith family. We experience pastoral care and celebrate milestones. We serve together in various ministries both within the church and in the wider community. Best of all, we do all this in an intergenerational community that allows for interaction and growth across the full lifespan—weddings and funerals, confirmation or baptism, expository teaching, shared meals, prayer gatherings, mission trips, retreats, community outreach, and so much more.

Getting hundreds of eighteen- to twenty-two-year-olds in one room to sing praises to Jesus is great, but it can never replace the need for an intergenerational gathering of those who prayerfully wait for God together. One of the major things missing in chapels is intergenerational friendship and mentoring. Older adults and young children have so much to offer college students. The reverse is also true. High schoolers need to see college students following Jesus. Children need to learn from college students. Older adults (like me!) are deeply blessed by the enthusiasm and vibrancy of college students. My heart swells when I see the pews filled on Sunday mornings with students from my university. While in class I am their professor, on Sunday mornings I am their sister and fellow disciple. We pray for one another and learn from one another.

Our church embraces college students as part of our DNA. We invite students to volunteer in many capacities (setting up refreshments, collecting the offering, writing curriculum and teaching Sunday school, preparing Communion, playing instruments, or singing on our worship team). Students serve on our mission council and show up on church workdays to weed or paint alongside other members. When they graduate, we celebrate. When they move away, we send them with our blessing. It's healthy and good for students to find a place in an intergenerational family of faith where their stresses and celebrations can be contextualized in a lifetime of faithfulness.

Yesterday during the worship service at our church, a three-year-old waved at a college student he knew a few rows back. He had a big grin on his face when the college student waved back. After the children came back from Sunday school, it happened again with a different kid and a different college student. My heart was full. These children know these young adults because they are part of community groups in which older and younger believers encourage each other in their walk with God. They have become family.

The single most important factor that will contribute to your spiritual growth in college is plugging into a church. Without it you risk losing the habit that is most essential to a lifetime of discipleship.

A TALE OF TWO FAMILIES

A common mistake is to read our own cultural values into the Bible, seeing what we want to see. These days in the West the danger is to read the extension of the gospel message to Gentiles as a call to be radically inclusive, as though anyone is now welcome with no parameters, and the uniqueness of Israel's history no longer matters. However, to conclude that is to misread the New Testament. Another snippet from John's letters will make this clear. Just after reiterating the need to "love one another," he writes, "If anyone comes to you and does not bring this teaching, do not take them into your house or welcome them. Anyone who welcomes them shares in their wicked work" (2 John 10-11). God's family is open only to those who are walking in the truth. False teaching and false worship disqualify someone from membership in God's family.

For John, the call to walk in love does not mean anything goes. We've already seen how Paul's missionary work puts him at odds with many Jewish and pagan communities. Jesus himself says that he has not come to bring peace but a sword. The Bible's declaration that God is forming a family of faith in which we are invited to participate does not entail the erasure of boundaries. On the contrary, to become part of God's family enlists us in the greatest cosmic conflict of all. We are to be a "holy people," set apart from the world.

Jude warned about those who would infiltrate the church while following "their own ungodly desires" (Jude 18). In other words, we need to be on our guard against the dangers of absorbing worldly or ungodly values. We're being built into a temple for the indwelling Holy Spirit, which means it matters a great deal how we live.

The church challenges the prevailing human values of the day, but it also challenges demonic strongholds that animate those values. Just as the church is the means by which God intends to unite humanity under his rule, it is also how God plans to defeat the spiritual powers that oppose his rule. Marva Dawn writes, "The realm of the powers is of interest to the New Testament authors only because they must be resisted, because the authors are sure that in the victory of Christ their own ability to withstand the powers is assured, and because the Church is now the realm through which the powers continue to be defeated and by which their final end is foreshadowed."[11] Way more is at stake when we decide whether to join a church than we often realize.

> The church is the means by which God intends to unite humanity under his rule. It is also how God plans to defeat the spiritual powers that oppose his rule.

This is not to say that we should stockpile weapons. Dawn goes on to explain, "To counteract the principalities and powers requires a battle, but one that is essentially and entirely nonviolent because it is against the powers and never against the people who might be aligned with them. . . . The battle requires our active engagement, but is always God's work through our weakness."[12] We can see this in Ephesians 3:10, where Paul unveils what has been long hidden: "His intent was that now, through the church, the manifold wisdom of God should be made known to the rulers and authorities in the heavenly realms." The mysterious wisdom of God's administration of the universe is evident in the community gathered to worship his name. We bear witness to another way of being in the world.

The path to victory is characterized by servanthood (Mark 10:42-45). Following the example of Christ, who laid down his life on behalf of others, we participate in God's kingdom purposes to tear down strongholds opposed to his rule. As Paul writes, "Our struggle is not against flesh and blood, but against the rulers, against the authorities, against the powers of this dark world and against the spiritual forces of evil in the heavenly realms" (Ephesians 6:12). By standing firm in the faith, united with other believers, we push back against the darkness that threatens to take this world captive.

Revelation 21:3 presents the ultimate vision of God living among all those who bear his name in the new Jerusalem. We are fellow heirs of his kingdom. One of the most arresting images in John's vision is the unveiling of allegiances. Everyone John sees is either branded with God's name or the mark of the beast (Revelation 13:16-17; 14:1). As it turns out, the world is divided between two families—not based on ethnicity, but on allegiance. One family relates to God as Father, living as his children and heirs, and another family is set up in opposition to God, having allied itself with the power of the devil. Rome may appear to be supreme, but in John's vision, allegiance to Rome or any worldly system amounts to insurrection against the true King of the world.

JOINING THE CHOIR

On our own we can only do so much. Our passion wanes. Our energy fades. Humanly speaking, we can have all the best intentions, but we need each other to help us keep our eyes on Jesus. Institutions like churches have their problems, but there's no getting around the need for them.

One person cannot build a society alone. An individual cannot fill all the necessary roles for leadership, food, shelter, security, education, health care, transportation, trade, infrastructure, and the arts. Even pioneers relied on one another for plowing, barn raising, medical care (such as childbirth), and trade. To deny ourselves participation in the family of faith is to deny ourselves—and others—the collaboration we need to sustain the mission of God's people in the world.

We attended a magnificent choral concert recently at Biola University. A single vocalist, no matter how talented they are, is unable to produce the full and complex harmonies of a choir. A range of voices is required that spans several octaves. Everyone must be present, practiced, and paying attention, taking their cues from the director so that the whole choir can sing in sync. One of the remarkable things about a choir is that it can hold a note much longer than any individual. As each singer runs out of breath, they can take a quick breath and then rejoin the note. The collective effort carries the note without any discernible interruption. In other words, a choir is more than the sum of its individual parts.

This is also true of the church. Together we can hold a note long and full for centuries, with each of us taking a breath when we need to, knowing that the whole note does not depend on any one person. It's a relief knowing that I don't sustain all that is good and necessary in this life. I am part of something much bigger than myself. My voice matters, but mine is not the only voice. I was designed for collaboration with others. Any of us has a day or a week or a month or even a year where we are out of commission. Humans have limits. But together, we can take turns filling in for others who need to take a break or catch their breath. By receiving one another as gifts for our edification, we experience the fullness of what God intended for us. The presence of God in our midst makes our collective witness more than the sum of its parts.

I began this book with the story of my own official entrance into the church as an eleven-year-old girl. I close with the story of an adult man. God works through a myriad of circumstances to draw us to himself and to other believers so that we become part of his family.

In 2024, Hurricane Helene hit the home of Kate Shellnutt, editor at *Christianity Today* magazine. While that may seem like a tragedy, that's not how her husband Troy saw it. Kate writes,

> This year, our home and cars were hit by Hurricane Helene, with 16 trees falling on our roof and yard. Once the sun came up, my husband climbed over branches and stood in front of our house grinning. Three weeks before, he had come to faith. "I would be so mad if I hadn't found Jesus." It was providence, he said, that he wasn't worried about his car, his house, or his collectibles, now getting soggy in a room impaled by tree branches. Maybe this was his chance to get rid of possessions to follow Christ. Neither of us had Christian upbringings, but I found God when we were engaged and prayed for years that he would too. He supported me, celebrated my accomplishments at *Christianity Today*, and didn't belittle my beliefs—but never joined me at church.
>
> Late last summer, seemingly out of nowhere, he ordered a Bible and started in Matthew. He mainlined Bible podcasts. He began quoting Scripture in conversation, asking me about the

Trinity, and talking about Jesus. When he professed faith, I was shocked. Maybe too shocked. I realized that I had never thought God would actually grant the thing I'd been praying twelve years for. Or that it could happen like this, so suddenly, so fully. But he had.

My husband read from the Sermon at the Mount at our church days after the storm. He was baptized the next week. We saw our church come around us in the aftermath, letting us live in their homes and borrow their cars. We felt like we'd experienced the kingdom of heaven on earth, and it cemented my husband's faith and made him fall in love with the church like I had. My husband is a new person. He has continued to preach the gospel to me and encourage me daily since, even as we navigate displacement and rebuilding. The joy of this season has so far outweighed our losses.[13]

God established the church as a community of his followers who show allegiance to his rule and carry on his work in the world. Together we testify to the gracious work he accomplished in his Son, Jesus the Messiah, who made it possible for us to join this international, intergenerational family of faith that spans history, makes history, and brings history to its goal with one surprise after another. Together we defeat the darkness by participating in the reign of God and cultivating servanthood and humility. By receiving God's sacrificial love for us and by expressing that love to one another, we participate in God's one and only plan to restore creation and fulfill his covenant promises. Above all, the Spirit of God is present among us as we are united in Christ to one another.

Ironically, the church is an institution oriented around the truth of what it *cannot* do. Even if we all pitch in, volunteering our hearts out and giving generously, we cannot redeem the world. We gather in worship to recognize that we need God's intervention. We need the surprising work of transformation that only the Spirit can bring. So we gather and wait together for God to make all things new. Bit by bit he does that work as we show up to watch and wait and pray. I don't know about you, but this is one thing I do not want to miss.

Where and with whom do you plan to worship this week?

KEY IDEAS

- On our own, any one of us is incomplete. We are meant to join with others to become something more than we can be by ourselves. The presence of God in our midst makes our collective witness more than the sum of its parts.

- The family of God is not open to everyone. Membership is limited to those who have surrendered their lives to Jesus and who walk in the truth.

- To cultivate family bonds with other believers requires generosity and affection.

- To become part of God's family enlists us in the greatest cosmic conflict of all. By standing firm in the faith, united with other believers, we push back against the darkness that threatens to take this world captive.

DIGGING DEEPER

Jim Davis and Michael Graham with Ryan P. Burge. *The Great Dechurching: Who's Leaving, Why Are They Going, and What Will It Take to Bring Them Back?* Zondervan, 2023.

Marva J. Dawn. *Powers, Weakness, and the Tabernacling of God.* Eerdmans, 2001.

Christa L. McKirland. *God's Provision, Humanity's Need: The Gift of Our Dependence.* Baker Academic, 2022.

Scot McKnight and Laura Barringer. *A Church Called Tov: Forming a Goodness Culture That Resists Abuses of Power and Promotes Healing.* Tyndale, 2020.

Scot McKnight and Laura Barringer. *PIVOT: The Priorities, Practices, and Powers that Can Transform Your Church into a Tov Culture.* Tyndale, 2023.

Amy Peeler. *Hebrews.* Commentaries for Christian Formation. Eerdmans, 2024.

James K. A. Smith. *You Are What You Love: The Spiritual Power of Habit.* Brazos, 2016.

Related videos from BibleProject: "Hebrews," "Revelation 1–11," and "The Royal Priesthood."

ACKNOWLEDGMENTS

Stories are the best part of writing and reading. I'd like to say a special thank you to those who gave me permission to include their stories, including Daniel, Dad, Mom, Easton, Willy and Angela, Phil and Julie, Kate and Troy, Kevin, Mike, and Charlene. Knowing each of you and your stories (even the hard ones) has made my life richer.

A group of friends volunteered to read an earlier draft of the book and gave such helpful feedback: Blake and Tashi Widmer, Mike Davis, Brian Pollock, Carey Griffel, Pete Santucci, Daniel Imes, and my teaching assistants, Antracia Moorings and Serena Shu. Thanks for removing roadblocks for other readers! Antracia also helpfully drafted the discussion questions for me.

I'm so grateful for the outstanding team at IVP Academic, including my editor, Rachel Hastings, marketing guru, Alexandra Horn, publisher, Terumi Echols, my expert reviewer, Noel Forlini Burt, and all those working behind the scenes on cover design, page layouts, copyediting, distribution, sales, and publicity. Thanks for the honor of working with you again to bring another book into the world! In the process, I feel like we've become family.

Talbot School of Theology at Biola University is a wonderful place to work. I'm grateful for the steady support of my department chair, Charlie Trimm, and my deans Ed Stetzer, Scott Rae, and Doug Huffman for my research and writing projects. This project was finished during my research leave in the fall of 2024, which was jointly funded by Talbot and by a generous provost grant from Dr. Matthew Hall.

My husband, Daniel, urged me to write this book. He's been supportive from beginning to end. For over twenty-six years we've lived out of our core conviction that the church matters. Thank you, honey, for the more than 1,352 Sunday mornings (minus Covid and the occasional camping trip) where you have joined me in getting up and out the door to join other believers in worship and waiting. You have persevered with me when the sermons didn't float your boat and when you felt invisible and when sleeping in would have been nice. I don't take it for granted that we get to be part of God's family together.

We're both thankful for the churches that have become family for us, and to the pastors and worship leaders and Sunday school teachers and small group leaders who have invested so deeply in our flourishing as followers of Jesus.

Finally, to you, dear reader. In a world where innumerable things are vying for your attention, I'm honored that you have taken the time to hear what I have to say. You are the reason I write. The church is not complete without you. I hope your investment in reading will pay dividends for years to come!

APPENDIX: RESOURCES FROM BIBLEPROJECT

1 THE FAMILY OF ABRAHAM

"Temple"
BibleProject
www.ivpress.com/imes66

"The Covenants"
BibleProject
www.ivpress.com/imes67

"Blessing and Curse"
BibleProject
www.ivpress.com/imes68

2 GROWING PAINS

"Joshua"
BibleProject
www.ivpress.com/imes69

"Judges"
BibleProject
www.ivpress.com/imes70

"Ruth"
BibleProject
www.ivpress.com/imes71

3 FAMILY DYSFUNCTION

"Justice"
BibleProject
www.ivpress.com/imes72

"Generosity"
BibleProject
www.ivpress.com/imes73

"1 & 2 Kings"
BibleProject
www.ivpress.com/imes74

4 DIVIDED FAMILY

"The Prophets"
BibleProject
www.ivpress.com/imes75

"Public Reading of Scripture"
BibleProject
www.ivpress.com/imes76

5 KICKED OUT OF THE HOUSE

"Apocalyptic Literature"
BibleProject
www.ivpress.com/imes77

"Gospel of the Kingdom"
BibleProject
www.ivpress.com/imes78

"The Way of the Exile"
BibleProject
www.ivpress.com/imes79

6 PROCESSING FAMILY TRAUMA

"Psalms"
BibleProject
www.ivpress.com/imes80

"The Book of Psalms"
BibleProject
www.ivpress.com/imes81

"Lamentations"
BibleProject
www.ivpress.com/imes82

7 FAMILY DRAMA

"Ezra-Nehemiah"
BibleProject
www.ivpress.com/imes83

"1 & 2 Chronicles"
BibleProject
www.ivpress.com/imes84

"Holy Spirit"
BibleProject
www.ivpress.com/imes85

8 FAMILY REUNION

"Acts 1–12"
BibleProject
www.ivpress.com/imes86

"Generosity"
BibleProject
www.ivpress.com/imes87

"Anointing"
BibleProject
www.ivpress.com/imes88

9 THE FAMILY BUSINESS

"Romans 1–4"
BibleProject
www.ivpress.com/imes89

"The Last Will Be First"
BibleProject
www.ivpress.com/imes90

10 A NEW TEMPLE

"Hebrews"
BibleProject
www.ivpress.com/imes91

"Revelation 1–11"
BibleProject
www.ivpress.com/imes92

"The Royal Priesthood"
BibleProject
www.ivpress.com/imes93

DISCUSSION QUESTIONS

INTRODUCTION

Read Acts 1

1. The author says, "Many people assume that the church started on the day of Pentecost." In what ways is that version of church history misleading?

2. The Greek word *ekklēsia* is usually translated "church" in the New Testament. How was it understood outside the New Testament? What are the implications for how we understand the church?

3. Sometimes people think of the church as a self-help club rather than a family in which everyone can find a place to belong. What role has the church played in your life?

4. What prompted you to read this book? What are you hoping it will do for you?

1 THE FAMILY OF ABRAHAM

Read Genesis 11:27–12:20 and 15–16; Exodus 15

1. The author says, "God's promises transcend our personal lives." What, then, is the goal of God's promises?

2. Abraham's household is given "a surgical sign of their covenant with Yahweh." What is the connection between Abraham's circumcision and Sarah's barrenness?

3. The people of Israel choose to gather around the presence of Yahweh. Why do you think they choose to do this rather than uniting around their shared experience of slavery or some other commonality?

4. How have you experienced the presence of God in or through the church?

2 GROWING PAINS

Read Deuteronomy 14:22–15:11; Joshua 4; Judges 17–20; Ruth

1. According to the author, why is Deuteronomy an important place to discover our purpose as God's people?

2. List several ways that the "Sabbath year," or seventh year, reveals how members of God's church are to live like family.

3. In what ways have you seen church services incorporate all ages and abilities?

4. Can you think of ways that you've seen the church become a community for those who are vulnerable or weak? (Note: we're not talking about charity here, but true community that leads to belonging and full participation.) What barriers prevent this from happening more often?

3 FAMILY DYSFUNCTION

Read 1 Samuel 1–2 and 17; 2 Samuel 21; 1 Kings 8

1. How does the author explain Samuel's legal right to the priesthood even though he has no genealogical right to the role?

2. Explain the role food plays in 1 Samuel and why this is significant as a theme in the story line.

3. Do you have good examples of or ideas about how to handle the issue of intergenerational consequences for sin and subsequent restoration?

4. Restorative justice is the idea of making things right for those who have been harmed by a community. Have you seen restorative justice happen in your church?

5. In what areas of your life have you experienced God's presence despite your family's dysfunction?

4 DIVIDED FAMILY

Read 1 Kings 13 and 22; 2 Chronicles 20 and 34–35

1. Why did the nation of Israel divide into two kingdoms?

2. What were the benefits of King Josiah's gathering the people together to hear the words of Scripture?

3. King Jehoshaphat's honest prayer of desperation leads to him send out a worship team in battle instead of soldiers. What lessons can we take away from his example?

4. The church is at its best when it's collaborating in listening to and obeying God. When have you seen this in action? What did it look like?

5 KICKED OUT OF THE HOUSE

Read Jeremiah 29; Daniel 7; Ezekiel 1

1. Why did God inspire Jeremiah to tell the exiles to settle down in the foreign land of Babylon?

2. How do Daniel and Esther offer two models for navigating the life of faith in a pagan empire?

3. The author notes that "certain furnishings and people are missing from the temple vision." What's missing, and what do these omissions represent?

4. How can you better exhibit interdependence with your fellow Christians rather than celebrating your independence?

5. The author writes about a skateboarding ministry that reached hundreds of young people. What are some creative ministries that you've seen that have helped people to hear and respond to the gospel?

6 PROCESSING FAMILY TRAUMA

Read Psalm 74, 83, and 96; Isaiah 35

1. What reasons does the author give for prioritizing corporate worship?

2. How do praise psalms play a key role in maintaining national identity in the Old Testament?

3. Lament played a huge role in the community life of God's people. How can the lament psalms shape Christian worship and community today?

4. Have you seen Christian nationalism up close? When does patriotism cross the line into more dangerous forms of Christian nationalism?

5. How do you think about voting and other forms of civic engagement? Do you view your political involvement as the establishment of God's kingdom? Has this book altered or solidified your view on this matter?

7 FAMILY DRAMA

Read Ezra 9–10; Malachi 2; Haggai 1; Isaiah 58–59; 1 Chronicles 21

1. How did Ezra and Nehemiah's selective reading of the Torah result in unnecessarily harsh reforms for the people who returned to Judah to rebuild the temple and community?

2. What are the ramifications of excluding foreigners from the work and life of the Israelites?

3. In what ways does your mindset have to shift to see yourself as a part of the worldwide family of God?

4. The Bible describes a multiethnic community that waits for the presence of God and carries out the work he gave us to do. In what ways has your church experience aligned with this vision? If it hasn't, how would you describe your church experience?

8 FAMILY REUNION

Read Matthew 1; John 4; Acts 2 and 17

1. Why is it significant that God redefined family according to allegiance to Jesus as King rather than biological family?

2. The author states that "the Christian faith is always one generation away from extinction." Do you agree with this statement? Why or why not?

3. Jesus' genealogy includes several women—most of whom were non-Israelites—and his ministry includes significant meetings with a Samaritan woman and a Syrophoenician woman. Why is it important that Jesus' life story includes non-Israelite women?

4. The author notes that sibling relationships were primary in the first century. What would need to shift in your life if you took seriously the idea that fellow believers are siblings in Christ?

5. How can the church today facilitate the fulfillment of the prophet Joel's announcement that "your sons and daughters will prophesy"? What would need to change to see it happen in your church context?

9 THE FAMILY BUSINESS

Read Romans 16, 14–15, and 9–11 (yes, that's backwards on purpose)

1. What is the significance of Paul's long list of greetings at the end of his letter to the churches in Rome? What does it accomplish?

2. The author mentions that Jesus conquered sin and death but that crushing Satan is not a one-time event. How can the church participate in this ongoing mission?

3. How do you square Paul's restrictive comments in 1 Timothy 2:12 and 1 Corinthians 14:35 with his clear affirmation of so many women contributing to the ministry?

4. The author lists three scenarios when it would be appropriate to leave a church—rejection of scriptural authority, authoritarian leadership, or abusive behavior that is not properly addressed. Do you agree that these are valid reasons to leave? Are there others you would add?

10 A NEW TEMPLE

Read Hebrews 10; 2 John; Jude

1. How does the author of Hebrews encourage believers to keep meeting together?

2. How does fellowship with others have a bearing on how you experience union with Christ?

3. The author says, "To share in the sufferings of others is part of what it means to become God's family." Can you think of examples where you have seen this in action?

4. How is standing firm in the faith, united with other believers, more effective than pushing back against the darkness by yourself?

5. After reading this book, how have your views on what it means to be God's family changed?

NOTES

INTRODUCTION

[1] Mark R. Glanville, *Improvising Church: Scripture as the Source of Harmony, Rhythm, and Soul* (IVP Academic, 2024), 4, 93.

[2] Melanie Ross, "Evangelical Worship: A Conversation with Three Publics," *International Journal of Public Theology* 12 (2018): 178-94.

[3] Andrew Root, *Churches and the Crisis of Decline: A Hopeful, Practical Ecclesiology for a Secular Age* (Baker Academic, 2022), 75.

[4] Russell Moore, *Losing Our Religion: An Altar Call for Evangelical America* (Sentinel, 2023), 41.

[5] Jim Davis and Michael Graham with Ryan P. Burge, *The Great Dechurching: Who's Leaving, Why Are They Going, and What Will It Take to Bring Them Back?* (Zondervan, 2023), 3.

1. THE FAMILY OF ABRAHAM

[1] E. Randolph Richards and Richard James, *Misreading Scripture with Individualist Eyes: Patronage, Honor, and Shame in the Biblical World* (IVP Academic, 2020), 4.

[2] Mark R. Glanville, *Improvising Church: Scripture as the Source of Harmony, Rhythm, and Soul* (IVP Academic, 2024), 93.

[3] David A. Falk, *The Ark of the Covenant in Its Egyptian Context: An Illustrated Journey* (Hendrickson, 2020).

[4] Joshua Berman, "The Kadesh Inscriptions of Ramesses II and the Exodus Sea Account (Exodus 13:17–15:19)," in *"Did I Not Bring Israel Out of Egypt?": Biblical, Archaeological, and Egyptological Perspectives on the Exodus Narratives*, ed. James K. Hoffmeier, Alan R. Millard, and Gary A. Rendsburg (Eisenbrauns, 2016), 93-112.

[5] David A. DeSilva, *Honor, Patronage, Kinship, and Purity: Unlocking New Testament Culture*, 2nd ed. (IVP Academic, 2022), 274-75.

[6]Myles Werntz, "Church Is Life Together or Not at All," *Christianity Today*, September 14, 2023, www.christianitytoday.com/2023/09/dechurching -evangelical-church-bonhoeffer-life-together/.

2. GROWING PAINS

[1]Michael J. Rhodes, *Just Discipleship: Biblical Justice in an Unjust World* (IVP Academic, 2023), 49-50.

[2]Aaron's family serve as priests. Technically, Moses and Aaron are also Levites, but the term tends to be applied to those outside the priestly family.

[3]Rhodes, *Just Discipleship*, 49.

[4]Justo L. González, *Teach Us to Pray: The Lord's Prayer in the Early Church and Today* (Eerdmans, 2020).

[5]Emily Hunter McGowin, *Christmas: The Season of Life and Light* (InterVarsity Press, 2023), 29.

[6]This instruction in Deuteronomy 15 expands on similar laws in Exodus 21:2-11, which only allows male servants to go free because female servants married into the employer's family. Deuteronomy recognizes the possibility of temporary female servitude that does not involve marriage. Non-Israelites could enter long-term servitude, likely because they were ineligible for land ownership in Israel (see Leviticus 25:44-46). Their survival in the land depended on their attachment to an Israelite household.

[7]Thanks to Kit Barker for pointing this out in "Finding Phinehas: The Rhetorical Function of Dischronology in Judges 19–21" (paper presented at Institute for Biblical Research meeting, San Diego, 2024).

3. FAMILY DYSFUNCTION

[1]A man named Elkanah appears in the fifth generation from Levi (Korah's grandson), so we might conclude that this Elkanah is Samuel's ancestor. Alternatively, in 1 Chronicles 6:33-38, our Elkanah appears as a descendant of Korah through another son of Tahath named Zephaniah (rather than Uriel). It's all a puzzle to me because far too many generations elapse between the exodus and the birth of Samuel. We know Samuel was born before the monarchy, when local judges ruled, and his grandson worked in the temple under Solomon. The line of Aaron includes only six or seven generations of high priests before the rule of King David. The list in 1 Chronicles 6 includes twice that number of generations.

[2]Denise C. Flanders, "The Reversal of (Food) Injustice: The Song of Hannah (1 Sam 2:1-20)," *Bulletin for Biblical Research* 33, no. 4 (2023): 458-75.

[3]Flanders, "Reversal of (Food) Injustice," 460-61.

4Flanders, "Reversal of (Food) Injustice," 464.

5Noted by Flanders, "Reversal of (Food) Injustice," 469.

6Flanders, "Reversal of (Food) Injustice," 474.

7David G. Firth, "They Sang and They Celebrated: The Women's Celebration in 1 Samuel 18:7," *Bulletin for Biblical Research* 33, no. 4 (2023): 486.

8Christine Jeske, "Stop Looking Away: What an Obscure Bible Character Shows Us About George Floyd's Death," Cateclesia Institute, July 1, 2020, https://cateclesia.com/2020/07/01/stop-looking-away-what-an-obscure-bible-character-shows-us-about-george-floyds-death/.

4. DIVIDED FAMILY

1Noted by Peter Leithart, *1 & 2 Kings*, Brazos Theological Commentary on the Bible (Brazos, 2006), 96.

2Kenneth Ngwa's *Let My People Live* represents a modern attempt to do the same thing. He reads the golden calf episode as a resistance narrative to Moses' autocratic leadership. See Kenneth N. Ngwa, *Let My People Live: An Africana Reading of Exodus* (Westminster John Knox, 2022).

3Leithart, *1 & 2 Kings*, 98-99.

4Leithart, *1 & 2 Kings*, 101.

5Leithart, *1 & 2 Kings*, 161.

5. KICKED OUT OF THE HOUSE

1Esau McCaulley, "Loving America Means Expecting More from It," *New York Times*, July 4, 2024, www.nytimes.com/2024/07/04/opinion/patriotism-july-fourth.html.

2Thanks to Deryk Machado for this insight in his sermon on June 16, 2024, at Redeemer Church, La Mirada, CA.

3Jonathan Brooks, *Church Forsaken: Practicing Presence in Neglected Neighborhoods* (InterVarsity Press, 2018), 47-55.

4C. Christopher Smith, *Reading for the Common Good: How Books Help Our Churches and Neighborhoods Flourish* (InterVarsity Press, 2016), 15.

5Daniel I. Block, *The Book of Ezekiel: Chapters 25–48*, New International Commentary on the Old Testament (Eerdmans, 2003).

6. PROCESSING FAMILY TRAUMA

1Justin L. Barrett and Pamela Ebstyne King, *Thriving with Stone Age Minds: Evolutionary Psychology, Christian Faith, and the Quest for Human Flourishing*, BioLogos Books on Science and Christianity (IVP Academic, 2021).

2Parts of the following section are adapted from two online articles: Carmen Joy Imes, "The Politics of Praise—Psalm 148," Politics of Scripture, May 13,

2019, https://politicaltheology.com/the-politics-of-praise-psalm-148/; Imes, "Praising God Is an Act of Political Defiance," *Christianity Today*, July 24, 2024, www.christianitytoday.com/2024/07/psalms-praise-politics-worship-weapon-spiritual-warfare/.

[3] Walter Brueggemann, *From Whom No Secrets Are Hid: Introducing the Psalms* (Westminster John Knox, 2014), 42.

[4] Brueggemann, *From Whom No Secrets Are Hid*, 46-47.

[5] I've quoted from the NIV here but replaced "LORD" with the divine name Yahweh to help us experience the specificity of the original Hebrew in its context.

[6] This section is taken from my blog: Carmen Joy Imes, "The Sound of Music and the Audacity of Praise," May 17, 2019, https://carmenjoyimes.blogspot.com/2019/05/the-sound-of-music-and-audacity-of.html.

7. FAMILY DRAMA

[1] The following paragraphs are taken from Carmen Joy Imes, "The Torah Is Pro-immigrant. Nehemiah Was Not," Holy Post, 2023, www.holypost.com/post/the-torah-is-pro-immigrant-nehemiah-was-not.

[2] Jennifer Powell McNutt shares this story in her book *The Mary We Forgot: What the Apostle to the Apostles Teaches the Church Today* (Brazos, 2024), 124-25.

8. FAMILY REUNION

[1] Joseph H. Hellerman, *When the Church Was a Family: Recapturing Jesus' Vision for Authentic Christian Community* (B&H Academic, 2009).

[2] David Bennett, *A War of Loves: The Unexpected Story of a Gay Activist Discovering Jesus* (Zondervan, 2018), 252.

[3] Sean McDowell and Scott Rae, "A Compelling Vision of Friendship with Rebecca McLaughlin," Think Biblically, n.d.

[4] C. Kavin Rowe, *World Upside Down: Reading Acts in the Graeco-Roman Age* (Oxford University Press, 2009), 27-32.

[5] Rowe, *World Upside Down*, 39-41.

[6] Siu Fung Wu, *Finding God in Suffering: Journeying with Jesus and Scriptures* (Wipf & Stock, 2023), 62.

[7] Wu, *Finding God in Suffering*, 10.

[8] I owe the insights in this section to my New Testament colleague Dr. James Petitfils, who teaches a course titled Biblical Backgrounds and shared his notes and lectures with me.

[9] Emilio Alvarez, *Pentecost: A Day of Power for All People*, Fullness of Time (InterVarsity Press, 2023), 19.

[10]Raymond E. Brown, *A Once and Coming Spirit at Pentecost: Essays on the Liturgical Readings Between Easter and Pentecost, Taken from the Acts of the Apostles and the Gospel According to John* (Liturgical Press, 1994), 10. Cited in Alvarez, *Pentecost*, 39.

[11]I owe this insight to David Hoonpongsimanont in personal conversation.

[12]Alvarez, *Pentecost*, 37.

9. THE FAMILY BUSINESS

[1]Scot McKnight, *Reading Romans Backwards: A Gospel of Peace in the Midst of Empire* (Baker Academic, 2019), 16.

[2]McKnight, *Reading Romans Backwards*, 18.

[3]McKnight, *Reading Romans Backwards*, 41.

[4]Marva J. Dawn, *Powers, Weakness, and the Tabernacling of God* (Eerdmans, 2001), 143.

[5]I'm grateful to Joash Thomas, who brought this concept to my attention via Twitter and Substack. Ruth Padilla DeBorst identifies Donald MacGavren and Peter Wagner as some of its most notable proponents in her SeminaryNow course "Integral Mission."

[6]Al Tizon, *Christ Among the Classes: The Rich, the Poor, and the Mission of the Church* (Orbis, 2023). Tizon's powerful and challenging book includes an assessment tool for individuals, churches, and other organizations as well as case studies of those who have put these principles into practice.

[7]C. René Padilla, *What Is Integral Mission?*, trans. Rebecca Breekveldt, Global Voices: Latin America (Fortress, 2021), 8.

[8]Padilla, *What Is Integral Mission?*, 8. See also C. René Padilla, "The Unity of the Church and the Homogeneous Unit Principle," *International Bulletin of Mission Research* (1982): 23-30.

[9]Jason A. Staples, *Paul and the Resurrection of Israel: Jews, Former Gentiles, Israelites* (Cambridge University Press, 2024), 39.

[10]From Soong Chan Rah's course for SeminaryNow titled "The Church's Western Cultural Captivity."

[11]Staples, *Paul and the Resurrection of Israel*, 66.

10. A NEW TEMPLE

[1]James K. A. Smith, *You Are What You Love: The Spiritual Power of Habit* (Brazos, 2016), 77, 2.

[2]Smith, *You Are What You Love*, 38-46.

[3]Rowe, *World Upside Down*, 51.

[4]Amy Peeler, *Hebrews*, Commentaries for Christian Formation (Eerdmans, 2024), 279, 286.

[5]Noted in Dana M. Harris, *Hebrews*, Exegetical Guide to the Greek New Testament (B&H Academic, 2019).

[6]Christa McKirland, *God's Provision, Humanity's Need: The Gift of Our Dependence* (Baker Academic, 2022).

[7]I'm grateful to my colleague Rick Langer for pointing this out during a Talbot faculty meeting devotional during the 2023–2024 school year.

[8]N. T. Wright, *Into the Heart of Romans: A Deep Dive into Paul's Greatest Letter* (Zondervan Academic, 2023), 148.

[9]Wright, *Into the Heart of Romans*.

[10]Joseph H. Hellerman, *When the Church Was a Family: Recapturing Jesus' Vision for Authentic Christian Community* (B&H Academic, 2009), 87.

[11]Marva J. Dawn, *Powers, Weakness, and the Tabernacling of God* (Eerdmans, 2001), 29. She was drawing on Heinrich Schlier, *Principalities and Powers in the New Testament*, 13-14, 40, 52.

[12]Dawn, *Powers, Weakness, and the Tabernacling of God*, 131.

[13]Kate Shellnutt, X, December 24, 2024, https://x.com/kateshellnutt/status /1871603212794679482. Shared here with permission.

SIDEBAR NOTES

INTRODUCTION "BEING OR BECOMING GOD'S FAMILY?"

[a]E. Randolph Richards and Richard James, *Misreading Scripture with Individualist Eyes: Patronage, Honor, and Shame in the Biblical World* (IVP Academic, 2020), 240.

[b]Richards and James, *Misreading Scripture with Individualist Eyes*, 244.

1 "A MULTIETHNIC FAMILY"

[a]Although rabbinic tradition holds that they were younger half-sisters of Rachel and Leah by a different mother, it seems unlikely that family members would have been conscripted as slaves.

2 "CANAANITE GENOCIDE?"

[a]Jackie A. Naudé, "ḥrm #3050," in *New International Dictionary of Old Testament Theology and Exegesis*, ed. Willem VanGemeren (Zondervan, 1997), 2:277.

3 "MAKING AMENDS"

[a]Ian Austen, "'Horrible History': Mass Grave of Indigenous Children Reported in Canada," *New York Times*, May 28, 2021, www.nytimes.com/2021/05/28/world/canada/kamloops-mass-grave-residential-schools.html?searchResultPosition=1.

[b]Anderson Cooper, "Canada's Unmarked Graves: How Residential Schools Carried Out 'Cultural Genocide' Against Indigenous Children," CBS News, February 12, 2023, www.cbsnews.com/news/canada-residential-schools-unmarked-graves-indigenous-children-60-minutes-2022-02-06/.

[c]Brian Lilley, "LILLEY: Unmarked Graves Were Documented Years Ago but Most of Us Looked Away," *Toronto Sun*, July 7, 2021, https://torontosun.com/opinion/columnists/lilley-unmarked-graves-were-documented-years-ago-but-most-of-us-looked-away.

^dAs documented by Sean Carleton and Reid Gerbrandt, "We Fact-Checked Residential School Denialists and Debunked Their 'Mass Grave Hoax' Theory," The Conversation, October 17, 2023, https://theconversation.com/we-fact-checked-residential-school-denialists-and-debunked-their-mass-grave-hoax-theory-213435.

^eBrittany Hobson, "'New Journey': Pope Arrives in Canada for Visit Aimed at Indigenous Reconciliation," The Canadian Press, July 24, 2022, https://chvnradio.com/articles/new-journey-pope-arrives-in-canada-for-visit-aimed-at-indigenous-reconciliation.

5 "SKATE RAMPS IN CHURCH?"

^a"Ministry," Skate Church, accessed February 7, 2025, https://www.skatechurch.net/about/.

6 "UNDERSTANDING TRAUMA"

^aMichelle K. Keener, *Comfort in the Ashes: Explorations in the Book of Job to Support Trauma Survivors* (IVP Academic, 2025), 16.

^bKeener, *Comfort in the Ashes*, 31.

6 "THE PROBLEM WITH CHRISTIAN NATIONALISM"

^aDefinition developed with help from Caleb Campbell, *Disarming Leviathan: Loving Your Christian Nationalist Neighbor* (IVP Academic, 2024).

^bRussell Moore, *Losing Our Religion: An Altar Call for Evangelical America* (Sentinel, 2023), 117.

^cAngukali Rotokha, "Exodus and Liberation: Naga Nationalism and the People of God," in *Exploring the Old Testament in Asia: Evangelical Perspectives*, ed. Jerry Hwang and Angukali Rotokha, Foundations in Asian Christian Thought (Langham Global Library, 2022), 185-204.

^dDominique DuBois Gilliard, *Subversive Witness: Scripture's Call to Leverage Privilege* (Zondervan, 2021), 90.

^eI'm grateful to Joseph Leeds for this insight, shared during the Q&A at the Center for Pastor Theologians conference in September 2024.

7 "CAN WE CRITIQUE THE BIBLE?"

^aFor this argument, see J. Richard Middleton, *Abraham's Silence: The Binding of Isaac, the Suffering of Job, and How to Talk Back to God* (Baker Academic, 2021).

8 "CHILDREN AMONG THE DISCIPLES"

[a]Robbie F. Castleman, *Parenting in the Pew: Guiding Your Children into the Joy of Worship*, rev. ed. (InterVarsity Press, 2013).

[b]"Sunday Worship," New Community, accessed February 7, 2025, https://newcommunitycovenant.com/sunday-worship/.

9 "WOMEN IN MINISTRY WITH PAUL"

[a]Kenneth Berding, *What Are Spiritual Gifts? Rethinking the Conventional View* (Kregel, 2006).

[b]Nijay Gupta, *Tell Her Story: How Women Led, Taught, and Ministered in the Early Church* (IVP Academic, 2023); William G. Witt, *Icons of Christ: A Biblical and Systematic Theology for Women's Ordination* (Baylor University Press, 2020).

BIBLIOGRAPHY

Allen, Amy Lindeman. *The Gifts They Bring: How Children in the Gospels Can Shape Inclusive Ministry.* Westminster John Knox, 2023.

Alvarez, Emilio. *Pentecost: A Day of Power for All People.* Fullness of Time. InterVarsity Press, 2023.

Austen, Ian. "'Horrible History': Mass Grave of Indigenous Children Reported in Canada." *New York Times*, May 28, 2021. www.nytimes.com/2021/05/28/world/canada/kamloops-mass-grave-residential-schools.html?searchResultPosition=1.

Barker, Kit. "Finding Phinehas: The Rhetorical Function of Dischronology in Judges 19–21." Paper presented at Institute for Biblical Research meeting, San Diego, 2024.

Barrett, Justin L., and Pamela Ebstyne King. *Thriving with Stone Age Minds: Evolutionary Psychology, Christian Faith, and the Quest for Human Flourishing.* BioLogos Books on Science and Christianity. IVP Academic, 2021.

Bennett, David. *A War of Loves: The Unexpected Story of a Gay Activist Discovering Jesus.* Zondervan, 2018.

Berding, Kenneth. *What Are Spiritual Gifts? Rethinking the Conventional View.* Kregel, 2006.

Berman, Joshua. "The Kadesh Inscriptions of Ramesses II and the Exodus Sea Account (Exodus 13:17–15:19)." In *"Did I Not Bring Israel Out of Egypt?": Biblical, Archaeological, and Egyptological Perspectives on the Exodus Narratives*, edited by James K. Hoffmeier, Alan R. Millard, and Gary A. Rendsburg, 93-112. Eisenbrauns, 2016.

Block, Daniel I. *The Book of Ezekiel: Chapters 25–48.* New International Commentary on the Old Testament. Eerdmans, 2003.

Brooks, Jonathan. *Church Forsaken: Practicing Presence in Neglected Neighborhoods.* InterVarsity Press, 2018.

Brown, Raymond E. *A Once and Coming Spirit at Pentecost: Essays on the Liturgical Readings Between Easter and Pentecost, Taken from the Acts of the Apostles and the Gospel According to John.* Liturgical Press, 1994.

Brueggemann, Walter. *From Whom No Secrets Are Hid: Introducing the Psalms.* Westminster John Knox, 2014.

Campbell, Caleb. *Disarming Leviathan: Loving Your Christian Nationalist Neighbor.* IVP Academic, 2024.

Card, Michael. *A Sacred Sorrow: Reaching Out to God in the Lost Language of Lament.* NavPress, 2005.

Carleton, Sean, and Reid Gerbrandt. "We Fact-Checked Residential School Denialists and Debunked Their 'Mass Grave Hoax' Theory." The Conversation, October 17, 2023. https://theconversation.com/we-fact-checked-residential-school-denialists-and-debunked-their-mass-grave-hoax-theory-213435.

Castleman, Robbie F. *Parenting in the Pew: Guiding Your Children into the Joy of Worship.* Rev. ed. InterVarsity Press, 2013.

Chalmers, Aaron. *Interpreting the Prophets: Reading, Understanding and Preaching from the Worlds of the Prophets.* IVP Academic, 2015.

Cooper, Anderson. "Canada's Unmarked Graves: How Residential Schools Carried Out 'Cultural Genocide' Against Indigenous Children." CBS News, February 12, 2023. www.cbsnews.com/news/canada-residential-schools-unmarked-graves-indigenous-children-60-minutes-2022-02-06/.

Copan, Paul. *Is God a Moral Monster? Making Sense of the Old Testament God.* Baker, 2011.

Crowder, Stephanie Buckhanon. *When Momma Speaks: The Bible and Motherhood from a Womanist Perspective.* Westminster John Knox, 2016.

Davis, Jim, and Michael Graham with Ryan P. Burge. *The Great Dechurching: Who's Leaving, Why Are They Going, and What Will It Take to Bring Them Back?* Zondervan, 2023.

Dawn, Marva J. *Powers, Weakness, and the Tabernacling of God.* Eerdmans, 2001.

DeSilva, David A. *Honor, Patronage, Kinship, and Purity: Unlocking New Testament Culture.* 2nd ed. IVP Academic, 2022.

Falk, David A. *The Ark of the Covenant in Its Egyptian Context: An Illustrated Journey.* Hendrickson, 2020.

Firth, David G. "They Sang and They Celebrated: The Women's Celebration in 1 Samuel 18:7." *Bulletin for Biblical Research* 33, no. 4 (2023): 476-88.

Flanders, Denise C. "The Reversal of (Food) Injustice: The Song of Hannah (1 Sam 2:1-20)." *Bulletin for Biblical Research* 33, no. 4 (2023): 458-75.

Gafney, Wilda. *Womanist Midrash: A Reintroduction to the Women of the Torah and the Throne.* Westminster John Knox, 2017.

Gilliard, Dominique DuBois. *Subversive Witness: Scripture's Call to Leverage Privilege.* Zondervan, 2021.

Glahn, Sandra. *Nobody's Mother: Artemis of the Ephesians in Antiquity and the New Testament.* IVP Academic, 2023.

Glanville, Mark R. *Improvising Church: Scripture as the Source of Harmony, Rhythm, and Soul.* IVP Academic, 2024.

González, Justo L. *Teach Us To Pray: The Lord's Prayer in the Early Church and Today.* Eerdmans, 2020.

Gupta, Nijay. *Tell Her Story: How Women Led, Taught, and Ministered in the Early Church.* IVP Academic, 2023.

Harris, Dana M. *Hebrews.* Exegetical Guide to the Greek New Testament. B&H Academic, 2019.

Hellerman, Joseph H. *When the Church Was a Family: Recapturing Jesus' Vision for Authentic Christian Community.* B&H Academic, 2009.

Hobson, Brittany. "'New Journey': Pope Arrives in Canada for Visit Aimed at Indigenous Reconciliation." *The Canadian Press*, July 24, 2022. https://chvnradio.com/articles/new-journey-pope-arrives-in-canada-for-visit -aimed-at-indigenous-reconciliation.

Howard, David M. *An Introduction to the Old Testament Historical Books.* Moody, 1993.

Imes, Carmen Joy. *Bearing God's Name: Why Sinai Still Matters.* IVP Academic, 2019.

Imes, Carmen Joy. *Being God's Image: Why Creation Still Matters.* IVP Academic, 2023.

Imes, Carmen Joy. "The Politics of Praise—Psalm 148." Politics of Scripture, May 13, 2019. https://politicaltheology.com/the-politics-of-praise -psalm-148/.

Imes, Carmen Joy. "Praising God Is an Act of Political Defiance." *Christianity Today*, July 24, 2024. www.christianitytoday.com/2024/07/psalms -praise-politics-worship-weapon-spiritual-warfare/.

Imes, Carmen Joy. "The Sound of Music and the Audacity of Praise." May 17, 2019. https://carmenjoyimes.blogspot.com/2019/05/the-sound-of-music-and-audacity-of.html.

Imes, Carmen Joy. "The Torah is Pro-immigrant. Nehemiah Was Not." Holy Post, 2023. www.holypost.com/post/the-torah-is-pro-immigrant-nehemiah-was-not.

Imes, Carmen Joy. "'Your Sons and Daughters Will Prophesy': Healing the Body of Christ by Restoring a Biblical Vision of Spirit Empowerment." *Journal of Spiritual Formation and Soul Care* (Fall 2024).

Jeske, Christine. "Stop Looking Away: What an Obscure Bible Character Shows Us About George Floyd's Death." Cateclesia Institute, July 1, 2020. https://cateclesia.com/2020/07/01/stop-looking-away-what-an-obscure-bible-character-shows-us-about-george-floyds-death/.

Katongole, Emmanuel. *Born from Lament: The Theology and Politics of Hope in Africa.* Eerdmans, 2017.

Keener, Michelle. *Comfort in the Ashes: Explorations in the Book of Job to Support Trauma Survivors.* IVP Academic, 2025.

Leithart, Peter. *1 & 2 Kings.* Brazos Theological Commentary on the Bible. Brazos, 2006.

Lilley, Brian. "LILLEY: Unmarked Graves Were Documented Years Ago but Most of Us Looked Away." *Toronto Sun*, July 7, 2021. https://torontosun.com/opinion/columnists/lilley-unmarked-graves-were-documented-years-ago-but-most-of-us-looked-away.

McCaulley, Esau. "Loving America Means Expecting More from It." *The New York Times*, July 4, 2024. www.nytimes.com/2024/07/04/opinion/patriotism-july-fourth.html.

McDowell, Sean, and Scott Rae. "A Compelling Vision of Friendship with Rebecca McLaughlin." Think Biblically, n.d.

McGowin, Emily Hunter. *Christmas: The Season of Life and Light.* Fullness of Time. InterVarsity Press, 2023.

McKirland, Christa. *God's Provision, Humanity's Need: The Gift of Our Dependence.* Baker Academic, 2022.

McKirland, Christa. *A Theology of Authority: Rethinking Leadership in the Church.* Baker Academic, 2025.

McKnight, Scot. *Reading Romans Backwards: A Gospel of Peace in the Midst of Empire.* Baker Academic, 2019.

McKnight, Scot, and Laura Barringer. *A Church Called Tov: Forming a Goodness Culture That Resists Abuses of Power and Promotes Healing.* Tyndale, 2020.

McKnight, Scot, and Laura Barringer. *PIVOT: The Priorities, Practices, and Powers that Can Transform Your Church into a Tov Culture.* Tyndale, 2023.

McNutt, Jennifer Powell. *The Mary We Forgot: What the Apostle to the Apostles Teaches the Church Today.* Brazos, 2024.

Middleton, J. Richard. *Abraham's Silence: The Binding of Isaac, the Suffering of Job, and How to Talk Back to God.* Baker Academic, 2021.

Moore, Russell. *Losing Our Religion: An Altar Call for Evangelical America.* Sentinel, 2023.

Morales, L. Michael. *Exodus Old and New: A Biblical Theology of Redemption.* Essential Studies in Biblical Theology. IVP Academic, 2020.

Morales, L. Michael. *Who Shall Ascend the Mountain of the Lord? A Biblical Theology of Leviticus.* New Studies in Biblical Theology. IVP Academic, 2015.

Ngwa, Kenneth N. *Let My People Live: An Africana Reading of Exodus.* Westminster John Knox, 2022.

Padilla, C. René. "The Unity of the Church and the Homogeneous Unit Principle." *International Bulletin of Mission Research* (1982): 23-30.

Padilla, C. René. *What Is Integral Mission?* Translated by Rebecca Breekveldt. Global Voices: Latin America. Fortress, 2021.

Peeler, Amy. *Hebrews.* Commentaries for Christian Formation. Eerdmans, 2024.

Reeder, Caryn. *The Samaritan Woman's Story: Reconsidering John 4 After #ChurchToo.* IVP Academic, 2022.

Rhodes, Michael J. *Just Discipleship: Biblical Justice in an Unjust World.* IVP Academic, 2023.

Richards, E. Randolph, and Richard James. *Misreading Scripture with Individualist Eyes: Patronage, Honor, and Shame in the Biblical World.* IVP Academic, 2020.

Root, Andrew. *Churches and the Crisis of Decline: A Hopeful, Practical Ecclesiology for a Secular Age.* Baker Academic, 2022.

Ross, Melanie. "Evangelical Worship: A Conversation with Three Publics." *International Journal of Public Theology* 12 (2018): 178-94.

Rotokha, Angukali. "Exodus and Liberation: Naga Nationalism and the People of God." In *Exploring the Old Testament in Asia: Evangelical*

Perspectives, edited by Jerry Hwang and Angukali Rotokha, 185-204. Foundations in Asian Christian Thought. Langham Global Library, 2022.

Rowe, C. Kavin. *World Upside Down: Reading Acts in the Graeco-Roman Age*. Oxford University Press, 2009.

Smith, C. Christopher. *Reading for the Common Good: How Books Help Our Churches and Neighborhoods Flourish*. InterVarsity Press, 2016.

Smith, James K. A. *You Are What You Love: The Spiritual Power of Habit*. Brazos, 2016.

Staples, Jason A. *Paul and the Resurrection of Israel: Jews, Former Gentiles, Israelites*. Cambridge University Press, 2024.

Strobel, Kyle, and Jamin Goggin. *The Way of the Dragon or the Way of the Lamb: Searching for Jesus' Path of Power in a Church That Has Abandoned It*. Thomas Nelson, 2021.

Tizon, Al. *Christ Among the Classes: The Rich, the Poor, and the Mission of the Church*. Orbis, 2023.

Trimm, Charlie. *The Destruction of the Canaanites: God, Genocide, and Biblical Interpretation*. Eerdmans, 2022.

VanGemeren, Willem, ed. *New International Dictionary of Old Testament Theology and Exegesis*. Zondervan, 1997.

Werntz, Myles. "Church Is Life Together or Not at All." *Christianity Today*, September 14, 2023. www.christianitytoday.com/2023/09/dechurching -evangelical-church-bonhoeffer-life-together/.

Wintle, Brian, Havilah Dharamraj, Jesudason Baskar Jeyaraj, Paul Swarup, Jacob Cherian, and Finny Philip, eds. *South Asia Bible Commentary: A One-Volume Commentary on the Whole Bible*. Zondervan, 2015.

Witt, William G. *Icons of Christ: A Biblical and Systematic Theology for Women's Ordination*. Baylor University Press, 2020.

Wright, Christopher J. H. *Exodus*. The Story of God Bible Commentary. Zondervan, 2021.

Wright, Christopher J. H. *The God I Don't Understand: Reflections on Tough Questions of Faith*. Zondervan, 2016.

Wright, N. T. *Into the Heart of Romans: A Deep Dive into Paul's Greatest Letter*. Zondervan Academic, 2023.

Wu, Siu Fung. *Finding God in Suffering: Journeying with Jesus and Scriptures*. Wipf & Stock, 2023.

SCRIPTURE INDEX

ALSO BY
CARMEN JOY IMES

Bearing God's Name
978-0-8308-5269-7

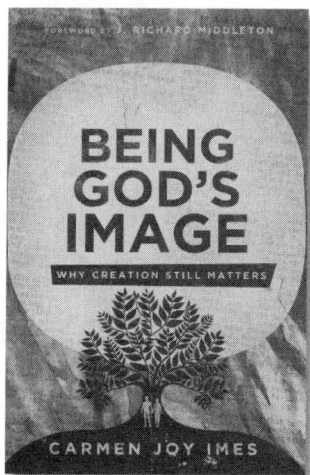

Being God's Image
978-1-5140-0020-5